THE

ART

OF

RATE

DESIGN

BY

FRANK S.

WALTERS

338.47621
W 235

© 1984 Edison Electric Institute
1111 19th Street, N.W.
Washington, DC 20036-3691

Printed in the United States of America
at Sheridan Printing Company, Inc., Alpha, NJ

ISBN 0-931032-19-9

ABOUT EEI

Edison Electric Institute is the association of America's investor-owned electric utility companies. Organized in 1933 and incorporated in 1970, EEI provides a principal forum where electric utility people exchange information on developments in their business, and maintain liaison between the industry and the federal government. Its officers act as spokesmen for investor-owned electric utility companies on subjects of national interest.

Since 1933, EEI has been a strong, continuous stimulant to the art of making electricity. A basic objective is the "advancement in the public service of the art of producing, transmitting, and distributing electricity and the promotion of scientific research in such field." EEI ascertains factual information, data, and statistics relating to the electric industry, and makes them available to member companies, the public, and government representatives.

ABOUT THIS SERIES

The ultimate responsibility for determining the fate of this nation rests with its citizens. Given that responsibility, they need access to the facts and knowledge essential to the decision-making process.

This series, *Decisionmakers Bookshelf*, represents one effort by Edison Electric Institute to provide U.S. citizens with the information they need to make wise decisions about national policy issues related to energy.

ABOUT THE AUTHOR

Frank S. Walters, an independent management consultant in the field of electric rate design and rate regulation, has had more than forty-five years experience in the electric power industry.

On July 1, 1978 he retired from the Potomac Electric Power Company [PEPCO] of Washington, D.C. after a distinguished career during which he held a number of key administrative and executive positions. He was vice president for Rates and Regulatory Practices and had previously served as manager of Commercial Operations.

Immediately after leaving PEPCO, he was retained as executive consultant to the Edison Electric Institute where he served as chairman of its Electric Rate Advisory Council. In that capacity, he was engaged in analysis and evaluation of the impact on the industry of the various ratemaking provisions of PURPA, the Public Utilities Regulatory Policies Act of 1978.

He holds the degree of Bachelor of Science in Electrical Engineering from the Massachusetts Institute of Technology and is a registered professional engineer. Before going on active duty in World War II, he attended the United States Coast Guard Academy, and is a Lieutenant Commander in the U.S.C.G. Reserve (Retired). In 1958 he attended the Public Utility Executive Course at the University of Michigan School of Business Administration.

He is a past chairman of the Rate Research Committee of the Edison Electric Institute. In addition, he is a charter member and first chairman of the Rate Section of the Southeastern Electric Exchange, and until retirement, was a member of the Load Research Committee of the Association of Edison Illuminating Companies.

An active participant in industry affairs, he continues to address industry related groups on many occasions. He participated in the National Rate Design Study under the joint auspices of the National Association of Regulatory Utility Commissioners, the Electric Power Research Institute, and the Edison Electric Institute, and was chairman of its Task Force No. 1 on "Analysis of Various Pricing Approaches."

He testifies before state and federal regulatory bodies on numerous occasions as an expert witness on rate design, rate application, load characteristics, load forecasting, cost of service and allocation methodology, as well as related policy matters.

TABLE OF CONTENTS

FIGURES

TABLES

ACKNOWLEDGMENTS

The author is deeply indebted to the five members of the review committee for their thorough study of the original manuscript and for the aggregate expertise embodied in their constructive criticism. They made many helpful suggestions for the manuscript's improvement. Profound thanks is extended to all of the reviewers who were as follows:

H. C. Allen, vice president, Research and Development, Union Electric Company, Saint Louis, Missouri;

A. J. Baldwin, asst. vice president, Division Operations, Pennsylvania Power and Light Company, Allentown, Pennsylvania;

G. R. Browne, executive vice president, New England Electric System, Westborough, Massachusetts;

W. J. Jefferson, vice president, Rates, Gulf States Utilities Co., Beaumont, Texas;

W. F. Schmidt, vice president, Rates & Regulatory Practices, Potomac Electric Power Company, Washington, D.C.; and

J. H. Ranniger, vice president, Rates and Regulation, Public Service Company of Colorado, Denver, Colorado.

Although it was not feasible to include every suggestion that was received, especially in those areas where there were differences of opinion among the reviewers, more than ninety percent of changes proposed were included in the final text of the book.

I am also greatly indebted to the members of the Edison Electric Institute staff whose assistance and encouragement were of great value to me throughout the preparation period:

David K. Owens, director, Rate Regulation Department, Edison Electric Institute; and

Peter Corcoran, policy analyst, Edison Electric Institute.

My appreciation is also extended to

Nancy H. Aronson, editorial consultant, whose constructive criticism has been extremely helpful.

I would also like to express my profound thanks to two outstanding industry leaders whose wise counsel early in my career was invaluable to me in the later years:

Alva B. Morgan, assistant managing director (retired), Edison Electric Institute; and

Leo Loeb, industry advisor and president, Loeb and Eames, New York, New York.

Last, but most certainly not least, I want to thank my very close friend of many years for his ever present encouragement, the late Thaddeus L. Sharkey of Ebasco Services. It was he who was largely responsible for getting me into the ratemaking discipline originally.

Frank S. Walters
June 10, 1983

Electric rates perform two vital functions. They set the price the consumer pays for service and are the means by which the utility generates its revenue. As the cost of doing business goes up for the producer, the price of the product must also rise if the producer is to make ends meet. Abrupt changes, quite naturally, cause some consumers to question their fairness. Customers face an increased financial obligation but find the rate structure a complex pricing mechanism that does not lend itself to easy understanding.

Electric rates must be "fair, reasonable, and not unduly discriminatory." These words set broad legal standards with which the tariffs must comply. What constitutes fairness, reasonableness, or undue discrimination is a matter of long regulatory history which is not set forth in this book. It is mentioned here only to indicate that a tariff must relate to the cost of providing service and that it must be equitable in its application to different types of customers. Obviously, it must produce the revenue for which it is designed and must be practical in terms of its applicability.

It is the overall objective of this writer to describe the rate setting process as we know it today in the interest of increased understanding of the art of rate design and the pricing of electric service.

Frank S. Walters

INTRODUCTION

Electric Utility Rate Design is intended to introduce a reader who is not knowledgeable about the electric utility industry to the process of rate design. The book is composed of three parts. Part I, consisting of the first four chapters, gives the reader background information that is essential to an understanding of the actual process of rate design, presented in Part II.

The first chapter of Part I, Overview of the Industry, introduces the reader to the operation of an electric utility, from the individual customer flipping a switch, to the power plant, to transmission, and ultimately back to the customer's meter.

The second chapter of Part I looks at the customer and how he uses electricity, and also, how the product is measured. With that information in mind, the reader is presented in Chapter 3 with sources of financial information essential to an understanding of the factors that are considered in the complicated process of rate design.

Part II, beginning with Chapter 4, takes the reader through the process of rate development. This part starts with costs and how they are reflected in rate schedules. The influence of time-of-use and different methods of costing are evaluated, followed by a discussion of the principles of load research and load management. Part II concludes with a look at the effect of adjustment clauses and other modifiers on rate schedules.

Finally, Part III, Outlook for the Future gives the reader some additional background information to the current rate development atmosphere, and looks at some emerging trends in the industry.

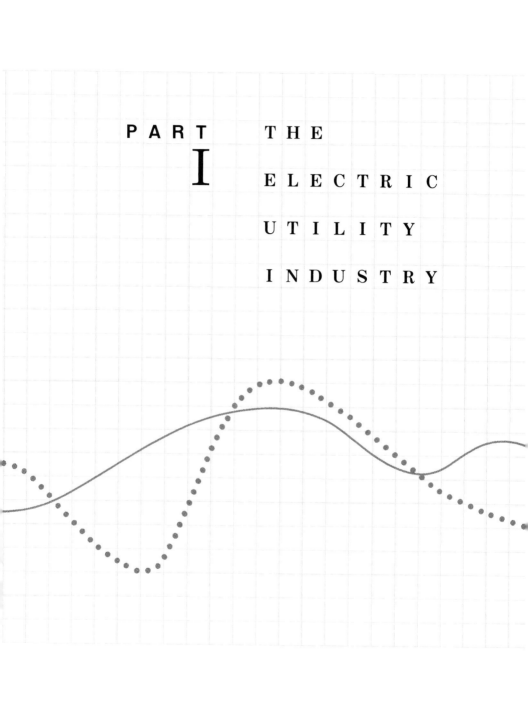

PART I

THE ELECTRIC UTILITY INDUSTRY

OVERVIEW OF THE INDUSTRY

The price tag

Ratemaking is the art of putting a price tag on the product furnished by a producing utility. When that product is electricity, the process differs substantially from the pricing function of other industries, even of other utility services. The differences in procedure evolve from the unique nature of electricity itself.

The nature of the product

Of prime importance is the fact that electricity, in the quantity required for utility service, cannot be stored. It must be generated and delivered within an infinitesimal fraction of a second of the time at which it is used by the customer. This response to the customer's requirement for service is essentially instantaneous since electricity travels at the speed of light, or 186,000 miles per second. Although these characteristics are obvious, they must be emphasized repeatedly because of their relevance to almost every step of the ratemaking process.

Technically, the electric utility must meet the aggregate peak requirement of its customers. If it does not, very serious operating problems are created. Because supply must be capable of meeting demand on such short notice, the utility's plant capacity must be at least equal to the maximum load that could be expected to be imposed at any one time, and its transmission and distribution facilities must be sized accordingly. However, to allow for unexpected variations in load, and for possible outages, as well as for equipment maintenance, additional capacity is necessary. This additional capacity is an essential requirement in that it provides the system with the flexibility needed to meet operating emergencies.

Customers are not all alike

Customer A flips a switch and the lights go on. His neighbor, Customer B, turns on lights, electric heating, an iron, a dryer, etc. Neither customer thinks anything about it. The power is there—for whatever the need.

Fortunately for the ratepayer, every customer does not make his greatest use of electricity at the same time. Differences in lifestyle and in use of household appliances result in diverse patterns of demand for electricity. For purposes of illustration, let us consider that Customer A's peak demand for power comes at 5:00 p.m., and that his neighbor, Customer B, does not reach his peak demand time until 7:00 p.m. In this example, the first customer's load may be decreasing as the load of his neighbor is rising to its maximum value. (Note that this example refers to residential use. Commercial, industrial and street lighting loads may all peak on different days and at different times.)

Coincidence of use

At the generating station, what is relevant in terms of the utility system is not Customer A's individual peak or Customer B's peak, but what is called the coincidence effect when those (and the loads of other customers) are combined. In this example, the greatest load of the combination would normally fall somewhere between five and seven o'clock, but its magnitude would be less than the sum of the two individual peak loads. Why? Because Customer A would be using increasingly less electricity and Customer B would not have reached his peak demand. The fact that the coincidence peak load would be less than the sum of the individual peak loads is of fundamental importance in rate design.

The combined load is the important factor at the generating stations, but at the point of delivery of service to the customer, conditions are quite different. For example, when an overhead service connection to Customer A's home is installed, the service cables, the electric meter for billing, and other electrical hardware items are selected solely on the basis of that one specific customer's pattern of use. Service to his neighbors does not pass through his meter since Customer B and other neighbors have comparable but separate facilities to supply and to measure the service. Unlike the situation of the power plant, there can be no joint use of the service connection facilities and no attenuation of demand because of diversity in utilization patterns.

At the line transformer, service typically might be supplied to ten or fifteen customers. The diversity in the customers' individual patterns of use is reflected in the degree to which their individual demands coincide in time of peak occurrence.

At other points on the electric system, the impact of diversity varies with the number of customers and types of applications involved. Broadly speaking, the effect of diversity is greatest when viewed from the point of generation, and least from the point of delivery of service.

The economic importance of diversity is easily illustrated by example. Consider a typical residential class load relationship. The maximum, coincident, combined load of all customers in that classification, on a winter day, typically might be as low as 40% of the sum of the maximum individual loads. Suppose all customers had their greatest use at the same time. (That would be a most unlikely occurrence.) The plant capacity would have to be two and one-half times as great, and the economic cost would be more than doubled.

Although individual customers' patterns of use differ widely, there is stability in the overall pattern when many thousands of customers are involved. Individual variations tend to average out so that a system load curve tends to have the same shape over a 24-hour period on successive days of the week. Naturally weekends and holidays are the exception. The magnitude of the daily peak will vary 10% or more from day-to-day because of changes in weather conditions, and other local factors which influence the use of electricity. However, the contour of the curve of hourly system load during the day tends to be reasonably repetitive on a seasonal basis, and operating plans of the utility for a day ahead can be largely based on this expectation.

Load variations

As previously noted, hour-to-hour variations on system load requirements are a direct reflection of the daily activities of people. During the period from midnight to a few hours before dawn, the load is low and is relatively uniform. It begins to increase as people awaken and start their routine of daily activities. When the peak load for the day is reached, the plant capacity needed to meet that requirement may be double or triple that utilized at three o'clock in the morning.

Loads may increase and decrease abruptly depending on the nature of the utility service area involved and the season of the year. The peak season for the majority of utilities occurs during the summer. There are, however, a substantial number of winter-peaking utilities. Although the characteristic load shape differs from utility to utility, there is a common operating problem at the power plant. The appropriate additional generating units must be put in service as the load builds up, and taken off the line as the load declines. Optimum scheduling of generators is a complex process, and an important one, from the standpoint of the economics of furnishing electric service. Today the actual scheduling of generators is largely handled by computer.

Generating procedure in the power plant

Variations in customer loads quite naturally require a response at the power plant in terms of the types of generating equipment needed to meet requirements at any given time.

Base load generating units supply large amounts of power and usually operate at or near full capacity for long periods of time. In terms of capital investment, they are the most expensive units. However, these units which are usually coal, nuclear, and less frequently oil, are the most efficient and, therefore, the most economical units in terms of operating expense.

At the other end of the scale are the power plant's peaking units. As the name implies, these units are not designed for continuous operation but are expected to operate during periods of peak demand, usually on only a few days, for a matter of hours at a time. A normal operating schedule might call for the use of peaking units for only 400 hours out of the 8,760 hours a year. These units, usually oil or gas combustion turbines or diesel, are the least costly in terms of capital investment, but are the most costly to operate.

Cycling or intermediate are terms applied to power-producing equipment which operates during those hours of the day when the system load has increased above the level carried by the base load machines, but has not reached the level requiring peaking units. Depending on load conditions at the time, they are not operated during the hours of lightest load on the system. These are usually coal- or oil-fired or hydroelectric units.

The economic contrast between base load and peaking units illustrates the fundamental problem of generator scheduling. While capital expenditure for a peaking unit may only be one-fourth of the outlay per kilowatt for base load equipment, the operating expense to generate a kilowatt-hour, using a peaking unit, may be four times the expense of generating it with base load equipment. Therefore, an optimum economic balance must be achieved in dispatching the utility's various generating units. Figure 1 shows a typical pattern of utilization of generation equipment in the three categories.

Delivery of power to the customer

Once the power has been generated by whatever combination of units was dictated by the load, the next step in the system is delivering the power to the customer.

Transmission and distribution facilities form the arteries through which power is delivered to the customer. In order to transmit electricity efficiently over distances greater than a city block or two, voltage levels much higher than normal are needed to minimize losses.

A number of different voltages are used by a typical utility. For example, generators in the power plant might operate at a nominal 13,000 volts. (Step-up transformers at that station might raise this to 230,000 volts for transmission and interconnection purposes, and

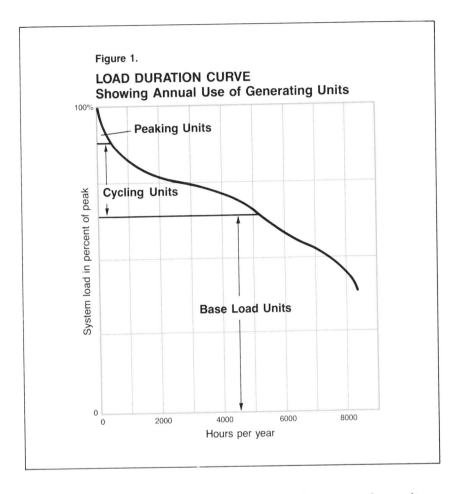

Figure 1.

LOAD DURATION CURVE
Showing Annual Use of Generating Units

Peaking Units

Cycling Units

Base Load Units

System load in percent of peak

Hours per year

feeders operating at 69,000 volts, 138,000 volts or at other voltage levels might form the major links between load centers and the generating stations themselves.) In turn, there are numerous distribution feeder voltages, from 2,300 volts up. The choice of voltage will depend on the density and type of load served, the mix of customers, and many electrical design factors.

Primary distribution lines operate at voltage levels from 2,300 volts to 22,000 volts or higher and are the workhorse elements of the distribution process. They deliver substantial amounts of power to key points throughout the service area where load is concentrated. However, in many instances, a primary line may extend for a number of miles to serve a relatively few customers in sparsely populated areas.

At various points adjacent to customer locations, line transformers are installed which reduce the voltage from the primary level to the utilization or secondary level, which normally ranges from 120 volts to 600 volts. Electricity is usually brought into the customer's premises by "service connection cables" operating at the appropriate secondary voltage for that specific customer.

High voltage lines generally cost much more to build than low voltage lines. However, using the same size conductor of electricity, the high voltage lines are capable of carrying much more power than lower voltage lines. Each level has its proper place in system design, but an economic and technical balance must be reached in each planning decision between power transmitting capability and the overall cost of plant.

Very large customers may be served at primary or transmission voltages with the customer providing his own transformers and associated auxiliary equipment. Rate schedules for such service make appropriate allowance for the equipment owned by the user.

Metering the service

Where those distribution lines reach the customer, billing meters are provided by the utility to measure the service furnished. This may be a single instrument to register only the kilowatt-hours of energy consumption, or it may be a complex combination of devices which also record the kilowatts of demand imposed by the customer at any time of day. Depending on the size of the load, and the nature of the measurements required, the cost of electric meters may be as little as $25 for a residential customer or may be many thousands of dollars for the equipment needed for metering the service to a large industrial plant.

Regulatory commissions

The service has been measured by the meter, now how much should the customer be billed? Here is where regulatory authority applies. Electric utilities in the United States are under the regulatory authority of both federal government and state government agencies. Retail rates, which are those covering service sold directly to the customer, are regulated at the state level. Wholesale rates, which cover the sale of electricity for resale by an intermediate party such as a municipality, a cooperative, or another utility, normally come under federal jurisdiction.

Capital requirements

Electric utilities are a capital-intensive industry. Investment in plant and equipment is three to four times the utility's total annual revenue. This contrasts sharply with most other businesses where the comparable ratio may be between one and one-and-a-half. In most cases, it is less than one.

In light of this intensive requirement for capital, it is quite understandable that one of a utility's major problems is financing. Securities must be sold in the market place at favorable interest rates to attract buyers. (Unfortunately, the time at which capital is needed is not necessarily the most favorable time for a sale of securities.) When there is increasing public demand for electricity, the need for additional plant capacity may make it impractical to wait for a better time in the market place.

Cost of money

The capital-intensive nature of this industry is recognized by regulatory agencies in the methodology they use to establish revenue levels. The utilities embrace the capital-intensive characteristic as a guiding principle in the technical design of the tariff itself.

Present day regulation of electric rates evolves from a determination of the cost of money in the market place. Once that cost is established, it is translated into an "allowable rate of return" on the company's capital structure, and rates are then designed to meet this cost as well as all other expenses incurred in furnishing electric service.

Since regulatory proceedings before commissions are quasi-judicial actions, any interested party may voice approval or disapproval of the rates proposed by the utility. The many legal actions in this process take time, and a formal proceeding may take more than a year to complete. In an inflationary economy, the time lag between application and approval of rate changes is an extremely important factor.

Rate of return

Unless rates are based on a fully forecast test year, utilities today cannot earn the "allowed rate of return" because of the increasing costs during the processing interval.

Reduced to its simplest terms, a regulatory cost of money formula might be the following: where financing consists of bonds, notes (55%), preferred (10%), and common stocks (35%).

	Capital Structure	Cost (Return)	Weighted Cost
Debt	55%	8%	4.4%
Preferred	10%	9%	0.9%
Common	35%	16%	5.6%
	100%		
Weighted Rate of Return			10.9%

The weighted rate of return of 10.9%, when applied to the utility's capital investment, after certain adjustments, would determine the dollars of return allowed by the commission. This amount, plus appropriate allowances to cover depreciation, taxes, and operating expenses, establishes the level of revenue set by the regulatory body. It would also be the target amount for rate design.

THE CUSTOMER'S USE OF THE PRODUCT

Service responsibility

It is an axiom of this industry that the amount of electricity furnished to the user and the time frame within which it is supplied are determined by the customer. The customer's pattern of demand is not controlled by the utility. In response to customer demand, it is the utility's responsibility to provide an adequate electricity supply—even at times of equipment failure.

Naturally, it is of vital interest to the utility company to know as much as possible about the patterns of use established by its customers. Analyzing these predictable patterns of use by major consumer groups is called "load research." (This technique is discussed in detail in Chapter 7.) Since electricity cannot be stored in quantities needed for utility service on a direct basis, the more information the utility has, the better it will be able to anticipate customer requirements.

The utility may try to encourage certain patterns of customer use. However, concepts of load control and load management are still dependent on customer response to price incentives, and/or to the use of load switching devices. (These may be used to disconnect some of the customer's equipment from the utility's lines at critical hours of the day.) In any case, the final energy requirement evolves from the customer's behavior.

Classes of customers

Patterns in use of electricity fall into three major categories. These are as follows:

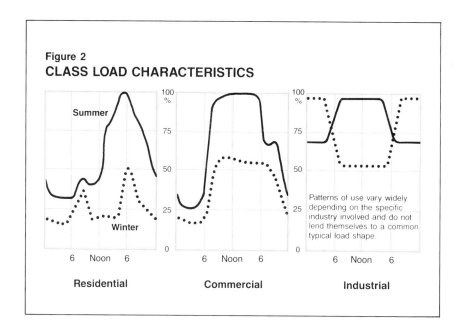

Figure 2
CLASS LOAD CHARACTERISTICS

Summer

Winter

100%
75
50
25
0

100%
75
50
25
0

Patterns of use vary widely depending on the specific industry involved and do not lend themselves to a common typical load shape.

6   Noon   6

6   Noon   6

6   Noon   6

Residential

Commercial

Industrial

- Residential Service
    Domestic occupancies including both homes and apartments.
- Commercial Service
    Frequently divided into small commercial and large commercial. Includes a wide range of business and service activities from the corner drug store to large hotels, apartment houses and other wholesale and retail businesses.
- Industrial Service
    Generally related to industry but may be similar to large commercial operations.

The broad objective is to consider those customers as a group who have reasonably homogeneous load characteristics, since rates are made for groups rather than individuals.

There are distinct differences in the patterns of use set by these groups. The characteristics of each of these components of the system load are illustrated in Figure 2 entitled "Class Load Characteristics."

System load curve

At the generating station, the aggregate electrical need of *all* customers served must be met and the system daily load curve (Figure 3)

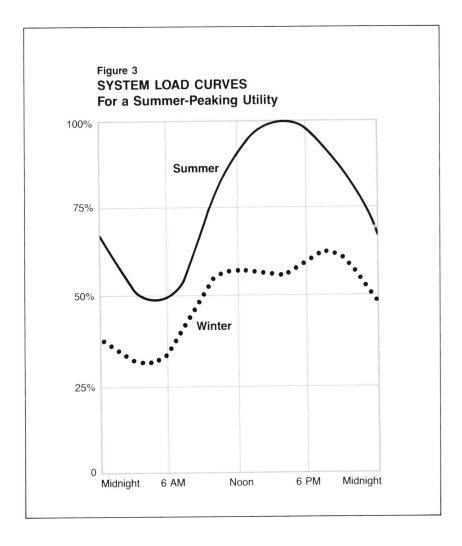

Figure 3
SYSTEM LOAD CURVES
For a Summer-Peaking Utility

is a graphic representation of this requirement for a summer peaking utility. As the curve shows, the summer load in this example is considerably greater than the winter load, indicating the large-scale presence of air conditioning. Generally speaking, such a utility would have lower daily peak loads in the spring and fall months. Unless the utility serves an industrial component taking service during off-peak or nighttime hours, the load will decrease during the evening and reach its daily low point at perhaps three o'clock in the morning. As daylight returns and business activity begins again, the load increases and the daily pattern is repeated.

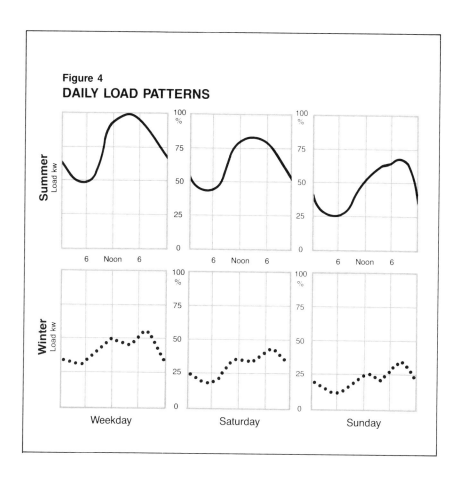

Figure 4
DAILY LOAD PATTERNS

Day to day patterns of use

There is considerable variation from day to day depending on differences in climatic conditions and other external influences. Saturday load shapes differ substantially from those experienced on weekdays. Sundays and holidays exhibit their own individual patterns of use.

A comparison of these characteristics is shown in Figure 4 where weekday, Saturday, Sunday, and holiday loads are depicted for both summer and winter seasons.

In order to meet these different daily load variations, the utility's schedule of use of its generating facilities must be planned in accordance with the probable pattern of use. At the same time, it must be flexible enough to take care of unexpected changes, either increases or decreases, as they occur.

Provision for maintenance

A very important aspect of generation planning is to make provision for equipment maintenance. Generators, turbines, and steam boilers require maintenance that keeps them out of service for as much as several months at a time.

In addition to scheduled maintenance, allowance must be made for the unexpected problems which may arise in case of equipment failure. Since the customers' loads must be met at all times, the expected load curve is of prime importance in the scheduling of generating units and in making proper allowance for servicing the equipment.

Measuring customer use—kilowatt-hours and kilowatts

The price of the electric utility's product for most customers evolves from two parameters of the service supplied—namely kilowatt-hours and kilowatts. A clear understanding of the distinction between those terms is of vital importance in understanding the rate design process.

By definition, the kilowatt-hour (kwhr) is the unit of electrical energy, and the kilowatt (kw) is the measure of electrical capacity.

Energy is delivered to the customer to perform a useful task. In most cases, the greater the task, the greater the amount of energy which must be supplied. Even so, the economics of delivering the energy is directly affected by the duration of the requirement and the manner in which it must be supplied.

Kilowatt not only quantifies the electrical size of generators, transformers, and other equipment; it is also used to evaluate the load which the consumer asks the utility to supply. Since electricity must be generated as needed, a one kilowatt load turned on by the customer requires one kilowatt of electrical capacity from the utility's system at the point of delivery.

Consider for a moment the elementary physics involved in the business of supplying electric power. If a consumer turns on a one kilowatt load and operates it for a period of one hour, the energy consumption would be one kilowatt-hour. It follows that ten hours of operation would require ten kilowatt-hours of energy. A load of ten kilowatts would have to operate for only one hour to consume the same number of kilowatt hours, (namely 10 kwhr). It is this interrelationship, between the kilowatt-hours of energy and the kilowatts of capacity required for its delivery, that is of vital importance in putting the price tag on the utility's product.

Keeping in mind that electricity cannot be kept in reserve, capacity must be supplied to meet the customer's maximum needs (kilowatts). In one sense of the word, this is like a rental charge on that portion of the utility's system which the customer requires. Yet this is a basic commitment by the utility which the customer may use in any manner which fulfills his individual needs. The degree of use that is made is dependent on the customer's mode of operation and is not under the utility's control.

Simply stated, the average price per kilowatt-hour a customer pays depends not only on the amount of energy consumed (kwhr), but also on its relationship to the capacity (kw) that the utility must make available for its delivery.

The load factor relationship

The ratio of the number of kilowatt-hours consumed per kilowatt of customer's load is the all important characteristic. When we speak of "hours use" or of "load factor," we are referring directly or indirectly to this relationship. Load factor is simply a measure of the average use of the service in relation to the maximum use made in the period of time involved.

In the interest of simplification, most rate computations are based on an average month of 730 hours, or one-twelfth of the 8,760 hours in a 365-day year.

If a customer were to sustain his one kilowatt requirement for the entire month, it could be said that he had made 730 hours use of his demand for capacity from the utility. It could also be said that he operated at 100% load factor because he had sustained his load uniformly during all of the hours of the period involved. If he consumed 365 kilowatt-hours during the month, he would have operated at a 50% load factor.

SOURCES OF DATA

Price and cost of electricity

Although many other factors may enter in, the price of any product sold in the market place evolves to a significant degree from the cost of producing and delivering that product to the purchaser. In the case of electricity, the pricing problem is further complicated because customers must share jointly in the economic responsibility for electrical equipment which supplies service to more than one consumer at the same point in time. This unique characteristic of the electrical utility industry gives rise to divergent expert opinions as to the appropriate costing methodology.

Many facets of cost determination are an integral part of the rate design process. Historical cost experience, as recorded on the books of the company, is referred to as "accounting cost" or "embedded cost".

"Marginal cost," defined in economic theory as the cost of producing one additional unit of output, goes beyond the basic accounting record and reflects cost that would be incurred if certain additional actions were taken. Marginal cost is also sometimes called "incremental cost" or "extra cost."

Until about fifteen years ago embedded cost methods were used for nearly all rate case computations. However, with a changing economic climate, marginal cost methods began to be introduced in rate proceedings.

Concurrent with this trend there has been a great deal of discussion and controversy about the relative appropriateness of the two methods.

It is not the intent of this book to make a detailed analysis of the economic theories involved. It is cited here primarily to call attention to the fact that many possible variations in costing procedures may be made. The particular one used in any given case will depend upon the specific utility and regulatory commission involved.

Today embedded costs are used to determine rate of return almost universally.

Marginal costs, modified to conform to revenue levels established on the basis of embedded costs, are used to indicate directions in which rates might be modified in the interests of economic efficiency.

The illustration of cost allocation procedure, set forth in Chapter 4, is reflective of embedded cost methodology. However, the examples of rate schedules which appear in Chapters 5 and 6 are based on assumed components of cost which could have been developed by either method.

As an objective, it is said that rates should be based on cost. However, rates do not track costs precisely. The rate designer must allow for many variables and must recognize reasonable differences in the methods used to assign the economic cost of jointly-used facilities. The initial source of data for cost development lies in the utility's accounting records and in its many financial analyses and reports.

Uniform system of accounts

For many years, utilities in the United States have operated under a Uniform System of Accounts issued by the Federal Energy Regulatory Commission (FERC) and revised from time to time as was deemed necessary to meet changing conditions. Use of the same account designations by all major utilities has enabled analysts of the industry to make meaningful comparisons; it has made regulatory procedures more efficient; and, it has provided the rate designer with a readily available source of cost data. However, primary accounting records provide only the initial data from which service costs are developed. Many additional analyses must be undertaken for rate design purposes.

Within the "Uniform System of Accounts," the sections of primary importance in rate design are the "Electric Plant Accounts" and the "Operating Expense Accounts," since these reflect the utility's investment in equipment and the outlay it must make for operation and maintenance of this equipment. (See Tables Ia and Ib.)

A chart showing the designation of electric plant accounts appears as Table Ia. Electric plant accounts reflect plant investment under five general categories as follows:

1. Intangible Plant
2. Production Plant
3. Transmission Plant
4. Distribution Plant
5. General Plant

A review of the specific account descriptions in each category (36 specific accounts under "Production Plants" alone) indicates the degree of detail by which costs are separated on the company's books. Nevertheless, many additional analyses must be made to provide the separation necessary for ratemaking. This is partially due to the "joint use" of facilities previously discussed, the need for such special analyses as a cost separation at different voltage levels, and the assignment of items to different classes of business.

For example, the cost of meters and their associated auxiliary devices are posted in account 370 "Meters". Installation on the customers' premises may range from a single kilowatt-hour meter in a residential structure to a highly complex industrial installation involving a number of kilowatt-hour recording instruments, demand meters which measure the kilowatts of the customers' load, instruments to indicate power factor, and a wide assortment of instrument transformers, relays, totalizers, and other special devices.

To make an equitable assignment of metering costs to a given class of user, an additional analysis is required assigning the costs of specific meters to the customer group employing that particular type of equipment. The importance of this analysis is illustrated by the fact that meter cost per customer may vary from $25 to many thousands of dollars for the largest installations where service is furnished at high voltage—69,000 volts or more.

Operation and maintenance

Operating and maintenance expenses are recorded in a series of accounts which closely follow the functional categories established for the electric plant accounts (see Table Ib).

Expense accounts are established for "production," "transmission," and "distribution" functions. However, additional provisions have been made for "customer accounts expenses" and "sales expenses" which are major categories of overall expense, but are not directly related to a specific category of electric plant.

For example, a review of the electric plant accounts will show that account 314 was established for "turbo-generator" units. The installed cost of such equipment is recorded in this account.

The corresponding provisions for expenses are covered by accounts 505 and 513, "electric expenses" and "maintenance of electric plant" respectively.

The instructions for account 505 read as follows:

This account shall include the cost of labor, materials used and expenses incurred in operating prime movers, generators and their auxiliary apparatus, switch gear and other electrical equipment to the points where electricity leaves for conversion for transmission or distribution.

Correspondingly, the following instructions cover account 513 for "maintenance of electric plant":

This account shall include the cost of labor, materials used and expenses incurred in the maintenance of electric plant, the book cost of which is includible in account 314, "turbo generator units."

As is illustrated by this example, the primary accounts provide the basic separation between the cost of equipment, the operating expense involved, and the expense of maintaining equipment.

In some cases, other items may be included. Electric plant account 314 relates only to steam-driven equipment, whereas account 513 (for maintenance) may include expenses associated with other types of equipment. In such instances, utilities may establish subordinate or subaccounts by adding a decimal point and an additional number to the account designation for identification purposes.

Table la
ELECTRIC PLANT ACCOUNTS (Chart of Accounts)

1. INTANGIBLE PLANT

301 Organization.
302 Franchises and consents.
303 Miscellaneous intangible plant.

2. PRODUCTION PLANT

A. STEAM PRODUCTION

310 Land and land rights.
311 Structures and improvements.
312 Boiler plant equipment.
313 Engines and engine driven generators.
314 Turbogenerator units.
315 Accessory electric equipment.
316 Miscellaneous power plant equipment.

B. NUCLEAR PRODUCTION

320 Land and land rights.
321 Structures and improvements.
322 Reactor plant equipment.
323 Turbogenerator units.
324 Accessory electric equipment.
325 Miscellaneous power plant equipment.

C. HYDRAULIC PRODUCTION

330 Land and land rights.
331 Structures and improvements.
332 Reservoirs, dams and waterways.
333 Water wheels, turbines and generators.
334 Accessory electric equipment.
335 Miscellaneous power plant equipment.
336 Roads, railroads and bridges.

D. OTHER PRODUCTION

340 Land and land rights.
341 Structures and improvements.
342 Fuel holders, producers and accessories.
343 Prime movers.
344 Generators.
345 Accessory electric equipment.
346 Miscellaneous power plant equipment.

3. TRANSMISSION PLANT

350 Land and land rights.
351 [Reserved]
352 Structures and improvements.
353 Station equipment.
354 Towers and fixtures.
355 Poles and fixtures.
356 Overhead conductors and devices.
357 Underground conduit.
358 Underground conductors and devices.
359 Roads and trails.

4. DISTRIBUTION PLANT

360 Land and land rights.
361 Structures and improvements.
362 Station equipment.
363 Storage battery equipment.
364 Poles, towers and fixtures.
365 Overhead conductors and devices.
366 Underground conduit.
367 Underground conductors and devices.
368 Line transformers.
369 Services.
370 Meters.
371 Installations on customers' premises.
372 Leased property on customers' premises.
373 Street lighting and signal systems.

5. GENERAL PLANT

389 Land and land rights.
390 Structures and improvements.
391 Office furniture and equipment.
392 Transportation equipment.
393 Stores equipment.
394 Tools, shop and garage equipment.
395 Laboratory equipment.
396 Power operated equipment.
397 Communication equipment.
398 Miscellaneous equipment.
399 Other tangible property.

Table Ib

OPERATION AND MAINTENANCE EXPENSE ACCOUNTS

1. POWER PRODUCTION EXPENSES

A. STEAM POWER GENERATION

Operation

500 Operation supervision and engineering.
501 Fuel.
502 Steam expenses.
503 Steam from other sources.
504 Steam transferred—Cr.
505 Electric expenses.
506 Miscellaneous steam power expenses.
507 Rents.

Maintenance

510 Maintenance supervision and engineering.
511 Maintenance of structures.
512 Maintenance of boiler plant.
513 Maintenance of electric plant.
514 Maintenance of miscellaneous steam plant.

B. NUCLEAR POWER GENERATION

Operation

517 Operation supervision and engineering.
518 Nuclear fuel expense.
519 Coolants and water.
520 Steam expenses.
521 Steam from other sources.
522 Steam transferred—Cr.
523 Electric expenses.
524 Miscellaneous nuclear power expenses.
525 Rents.

Maintenance

528 Maintenance supervision and engineering.
529 Maintenance of structures.
530 Maintenance of reactor plant equipment.
531 Maintenance of electric plant.
532 Maintenance of miscellaneous nuclear plant.

C. HYDRAULIC POWER GENERATION

Operation

535 Operation supervision and engineering.
536 Water for power.
537 Hydraulic expenses.
538 Electric expenses.
539 Miscellaneous hydraulic power generation expenses.
540 Rents.

Maintenance

541 Maintenance supervision and engineering.
542 Maintenance of structures.
543 Maintenance of reservoirs, dams and waterways.
544 Maintenance of electric plant.
545 Maintenance of miscellaneous hydraulic plant.

D. OTHER POWER GENERATION

Operation

546 Operation supervision and engineering.
547 Fuel.
548 Generation expenses.
549 Miscellaneous other power generation expenses.
550 Rents.

Maintenance

551 Maintenance supervision and engineering.
552 Maintenance of structures.
553 Maintenance of generating and electric plant.
554 Maintenance of miscellaneous other power generation plant.

E. OTHER POWER SUPPLY EXPENSES

555 Purchased power.
556 System control and load dispatching.
557 Other expenses.

2. TRANSMISSION EXPENSES

Operation

560 Operation supervision and engineering.
561 Load dispatching.
562 Station expenses.
563 Overhead line expenses.
564 Underground line expenses.
565 Transmission of electricity by others.
566 Miscellaneous transmission expenses.
567 Rents.

Maintenance

568 Maintenance supervision and engineering.
569 Maintenance of structures.
570 Maintenance of station equipment.
571 Maintenance of overhead lines.
572 Maintenance of underground lines.
573 Maintenance of miscellaneous transmission plant.

3. DISTRIBUTION EXPENSES

Operation

580 Operation supervision and engineering.
581 Load dispatching.
582 Station expenses.
583 Overhead line expenses.
584 Underground line expenses.
585 Street lighting and signal system expenses.
586 Meter expenses.
587 Customer installations expenses.
588 Miscellaneous distribution expenses.
589 Rents.

Maintenance

590 Maintenance supervision and engineering.
591 Maintenance of structures.
592 Maintenance of station equipment.
593 Maintenance of overhead lines.
594 Maintenance of underground lines.
595 Maintenance of line transformers.
596 Maintenance of street lighting and signal systems.
597 Maintenance of meters.
598 Maintenance of miscellaneous distribution plant.

4. CUSTOMER ACCOUNTS EXPENSES

Operation

901 Supervision.
902 Meter reading expenses.
903 Customer records and collection expenses.
904 Uncollectible accounts.
905 Miscellaneous customer accounts expenses.

5. SALES EXPENSES

Operation

911 Supervision.
912 Demonstrating and selling expenses.
913 Advertising expenses.
916 Miscellaneous sales expenses.

6. ADMINISTRATIVE AND GENERAL EXPENSES

Operation

920 Administrative and general salaries.
921 Office supplies and expenses.
922 Administrative expenses transferred—Cr.
923 Outside services employed.
924 Property insurance.
925 Injuries and damages.
926 Employee pensions and benefits.
927 Franchise requirements.
928 Regulatory commission expenses.
929 Duplicate charges—Cr.
930 Miscellaneous general expenses.
931 Rents.

Maintenance

932 Maintenance of general plant.

Table Ic
COST OF SERVICE STATEMENT

RATE BASE
Electric Plant in Service	$ 1,000,000,000
Construction Work in Progress	100,000,000
Electric Plant Held for Future Use	10,000,000
Materials and Supplies	30,000,000
Cash Working Capital	20,000,000
Accumulated Provision for Depreciation	− 200,000,000
Customer Advances	− 10,000,000
Total Rate Base	$ 950,000,000

OPERATING REVENUES
Sale of Electricity	$ 254,000,000
Other Operating Revenues	1,000,000
Total Operating Revenues	$ 255,000,000

OPERATING EXPENSES
Operation and Maintenance Expenses	$ 100,000,000
Depreciation Expense	25,000,000
Taxes	45,000,000
Total Operating Expenses	$ 170,000,000

OPERATING INCOME—RETURN
Revenue less Expense	$ 85,000,000

RATE OF RETURN (ON RATE BASE)	9%[1]

[1] 85,000,000 / 950,000,000 × 100 = 9%

Cost of service concepts

The starting point in rate design is a Cost-of-Service Statement, a simplified example of which is shown in Table Ic for a hypothetical utility with a billion dollar investment in electric plant in service. This document gives a statement of the rate base investment on which the utility is allowed by the commission to earn a return. It also gives a brief statement of the operating revenues and the operating expenses of the utility. The difference between them, of course, is the return. In addition to the dollar amount obtained by subtraction, the rate of return is obtained by relating the dollars of return to the dollars of rate base expressed as a percentage.

Return earned

Such a document may be prepared from accounting records without any adjustments and, done in this manner, the end result is the "return earned" for the period of time involved.

However, for rate design purposes, adjustments must be made to raise the return to the level allowed by commission decision. In the present economic climate, utilities seldom, if ever, actually earn the return allowed by the regulators, but instead are faced with a declining level of return over the passage of time.

Under these conditions, an increase in rates produces only partial compensation because the time required for the regulatory procedure permits further decline in earnings before the new schedules can become effective (i.e. "regulatory lag").

Revenue requirement

To initiate a rate change, a cost-of-service statement is prepared which reflects the level of return established by the regulatory authority. Based on that rate of return, revenues would be increased; taxes and other items would be adjusted as necessary to conform with the allowed level of return.

The dollars of revenue required after this adjustment become the "revenue requirement" for the rate proceeding. It is the target which all rate computations must support.

PART II

THE PROCESS OF RATE DESIGN

ALLOCATION OF COSTS

Having established the revenue target, the process of rate design moves on to the allocation of costs within the service area, and to the various rate classifications in each segment. It is a two step procedure.

Beginning with the investment in electric plant equipment, the allocation process analyzes and regroups investment costs as recorded on the books of the company. Transforming this recorded information from a tabulation by cost accounts to a tabulation by functional cost categories more nearly represents a breakdown based on the technical use of the equipment.

An illustration of a tabulation by accounts for the hypothetical utility is given in Table II and the tabulation of those costs by functions is shown in Table III.

Using the example on the account tabulation, the investment in production plant is $425,000,000, yet the power supply total in the functional tabulation is $500,000,000, or $75,000,000 higher. This difference is the result of the functional analysis. In addition to the cost of generating equipment itself, the power supply category also includes the cost of the major transmission lines and other facilities tying together the various power stations of the system.

It does not follow that all transmission lines between such stations are included in the power supply category. Only those lines which are absolutely necessary for the proper electrical operation of the generating system in an integrated manner are considered as a part of the power supply. The identification of these facilities must be made as a matter of engineering judgment by system planning and operating personnel. From a costing viewpoint, it is necessary to make such a separation because power supply and other facilities will be subjected to different treatment further on in the allocation procedure.

Table II

ELECTRIC PLANT IN SERVICE AS RECORDED BY ACCOUNTS

I INTANGIBLE PLANT			
301	Organization		
302	Franchises		
	Total Intangible Plant	$	—
II PRODUCTION PLANT			
	Steam Production Plant		
	Other Production Plant		
	Total Production Plant	$	425,000,000
III TRANSMISSION PLANT			
350	Land and Land Rights	$	10,000,000
352	Structures and Improvements		5,000,000
353	Station Equipment		75,000,000
354	Towers and Fixtures		13,000,000
355	Poles and Fixtures		2,000,000
356	Overhead Conductors and Devices		10,000,000
357	Underground Conduit		20,000,000
358	Underground Conductors and Devices		25,000,000
	Total Transmission Plant	$	160,000,000
IV DISTRIBUTION PLANT			
360	Land and Land Rights		10,000,000
361	Structures and Improvements		15,000,000
362	Station Equipment		40,000,000
364	Poles Towers and Fixtures		20,000,000
365	Overhead Conductors and Devices		25,000,000
366	Underground Conduit		65,000,000
367	Underground Conductors and Devices		60,000,000
368	Line Transformers		75,000,000
369.1	Overhead Services		15,000,000
369.1	Underground Services		25,000,000
370	Meters		20,000,000
	Total Distribution Plant	$	390,000,000
V GENERAL PLANT			
	Total General Plant	$	25,000,000
TOTAL PLANT IN SERVICE		$	1,000,000,000

Table III

ELECTRIC PLANT IN SERVICE BY FUNCTIONAL CATEGORIES

POWER SUPPLY
Production	$	425,000,000
Substations and Lines		75,000,000
Total Power Supply	$	500,000,000

SUB-TRANSMISSION
Substations	$	65,000,000
Lines		65,000,000
Total Sub-Transmission	$	130,000,000

GENERAL DISTRIBUTION
Substations	$	40,000,000
Primary Lines:		
Overhead	$	40,000,000
Underground		85,000,000
Total Primary Lines	$	125,000,000
Secondary Lines:		
Overhead	$	25,000,000
Underground		25,000,000
Total Secondary Lines	$	50,000,000
Transformers	$	70,000,000
Services:		
Overhead	$	15,000,000
Underground		25,000,000
Total Services	$	40,000,000
Meters	$	20,000,000
Total General Distribution	$	345,000,000

GENERAL PLANT .... $ 25,000,000

TOTAL PLANT IN SERVICE .... $ 1,000,000,000

In the General Distribution category, many functional totals are the same as the totals in the corresponding account record. An example of this compliance is illustrated by the Meters category, on Table III, in which the investment is the same in both forms of tabulation.

In other distribution categories, costs may be separated on the basis of underground and overhead facilities as well as by voltage levels.

The transformation, from an accounting to a functional statement of investment in plant, is only the initial step on the allocation process. Extensive additional analyses of costs are made as a part of the succeeding step in which the functional quantities are assigned to the jurisdictional and rate classifications within which the utility operates. (See Figure 5.)

In many phases of the allocation process, the assignment of costs is based on their degree of association with the energy, capacity, or customer-related functions of the electric system. For example, the cost of fuel is basically an energy item since the combustion process produces the heat which is transformed into electricity by the generating equipment.

On the other hand, the size of the generating equipment is dependent on the customer's peak load requirement, generally referred to as his maximum demand and measured in kilowatts. Investment in generating equipment is primarily a reflection of the capacity needed to meet that load.

Many elements of cost are not directly related to the number of kilowatt-hours of energy used by the consumer or to the capacity of the equipment needed to make the delivery, but can be related to the number of customers served. An example would be the expenses of meter reading, billing and collecting. However, an important segment of customer cost that does relate to investment in plant is the cost of minimum facilities needed for "readiness-to-serve" before any electricity is actually delivered to the user.

Importance of cost components

The concept of DEMAND, ENERGY and CUSTOMER components of

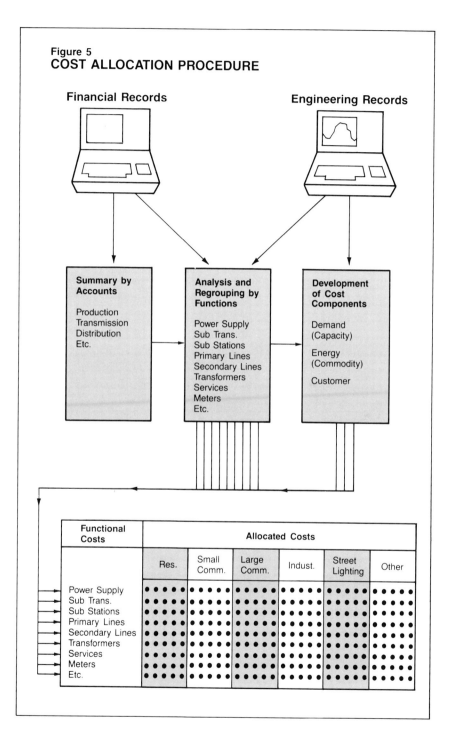

Figure 5
COST ALLOCATION PROCEDURE

Financial Records

Engineering Records

Summary by Accounts

Production
Transmission
Distribution
Etc.

Analysis and Regrouping by Functions

Power Supply
Sub Trans.
Sub Stations
Primary Lines
Secondary Lines
Transformers
Services
Meters
Etc.

Development of Cost Components

Demand
(Capacity)

Energy
(Commodity)

Customer

Functional Costs	Allocated Costs					
	Res.	Small Comm.	Large Comm.	Indust.	Street Lighting	Other
Power Supply						
Sub Trans.						
Sub Stations						
Primary Lines						
Secondary Lines						
Transformers						
Services						
Meters						
Etc.						

cost (D.E.C.) is used throughout the allocation process and, in turn, in the rate design procedure itself.

Prior to the allocation of cost between different regulatory jurisdictions and between classes of business or other rate categories, a preparatory step is the development of D.E.C. cost components. Once this is done, energy-related costs are allocated largely in proportion to the number of kilowatt-hours of energy consumed by each segment.

Costs are assigned on the basis of the number of customers served, after having first made direct assignments of those costs which are identified with specific classes of business or other groups.

The allocation of capacity costs is derived from the kilowatts of demand sustained. However, the kilowatt-hours of energy may also enter into the procedure depending on the specific method used.

Jointly-used facilities costs

Many different methods can be used to allocate the cost of plant facilities, such as generating equipment, that are used simultaneously by many customers. In actual practice, the choice is narrowed down to three or four procedures that have received regulatory recognition and general acceptance in the ratemaking process.

This choice in the allocation of capacity costs has evolved because electricity must be generated as needed. As many customers share in the joint use of electrical facilities, an equitable allocation of their costs involves not only the magnitude of the customers' loads, but also their duration. The relationships between the individual customers' patterns of use has a major bearing on the total system requirements.

There is no single, exact solution to this complex problem. Consequently, methods have been derived that produce results that are considered "fair and just" and not "unduly discriminatory" in the regulatory sense of those terms.

Although many methods have been developed for the allocation of "jointly-used facilities" costs, three methods are generally accepted in retail ratemaking at the present time. These are the following:

1. Peak responsibility method;

2. Non-coincident class peak method;
3. Average-excess demand method.
   (See detailed discussion in Appendix.)

Unit cost application

The demand, energy, and customer-related unit costs developed in the allocation process may be used as an initial step in price determination.

For purposes of illustration, these values have been applied on a system-wide basis. A single value has been assumed for each component. In actual practice, the cost allocation procedure itself develops and applies D.E.C. components at each functional level of the analysis. The final result yields a multiplicity of values for each component category.

Cost component relationships

To illustrate the basic relationship between D.E.C. components and price per kilowatt-hour, consider the following:

Assume that the costs given below are appropriate for residential service:

Demand Cost:	$8.00 kilowatt per month of diversified class demand
Energy Cost:	4.0¢ kilowatt-hour
Customer Cost:	$4.00 per customer per month

A typical residential customer using 800 kilowatt-hours per month might have a demand of 6 kilowatts measured at his meter. This would mean a load factor of 18%. (Remember, the load factor is equal to actual use in relation to maximum possible use.) However, because this typical customer and other residential customers differ with regard to time of use, his diversified or coincident maximum demand on the system might be only 3 kilowatts in relation to the class peak. This would mean a load factor of 36% based on the coincident demand per customer.

Using these statistics an application of cost components would indicate the following:

Demand Cost:	3 kw × $8.00	$24.00
Energy Cost:	800 kwhr × $0.04	32.00
Customer Cost:	1 customer × $4.00	4.00
Total Cost Per Month:		$60.00

Average cost per
kilowatt-hour: $60.00 ÷ 800 kwhr = $0.075 or 7.5¢

Vital importance of load factor

Except for the presence of the customer cost component, the resulting average rate is entirely dependent on the ratio of the number of kilowatt-hours used to the kilowatts of demand required to supply them.

In the example, if we consider *only* the demand and energy components, the resulting average rate would be:

Demand Cost:	3 kw × $8.00	$24.00
Energy Cost:	800 kwhr × $0.04	32.00
Total:		$56.00

Average per
kilowatt-hour: $56.00 ÷ 800 kwhr = $0.070 or 7.0¢

If we then assume that the customer uses twice as many kilowatt-hours and requires twice the demand to supply it, the cost calculation becomes:

Demand Cost:	6 kw × $8.00	$ 48.00
Energy Cost:	1,600 kwhr × $0.04	64.00
Total Cost:		$112.00

Average per
kilowatt-hour: $112.00 ÷ 1,600 kwhr = $0.070 or 7.0¢

This simple calculation demonstrates the importance of load factor in the pricing of electricity. In this case, there was no change in the unit price even though the electric service was doubled. The ratio of kwhr to kw was the same or, in other words, there was no change in load factor.

However, if the $4.00 per month customer cost is included in the computation, the cost when doubling the quantity becomes $112.00 + $4.00 = $116.00. With this included, the average cost per kwhr is $116.00 ÷ 1,600 kwhr = $0.0725 or 7.25¢.

Thus, the final average cost per kwhr for the 1,600 kwhr case is one quarter of a cent less, at 7.25¢, than for the 800 kwhr case where it was 7.5¢. Since there was no change in load factor, the reduction was due to the fact that the customer cost of $4.00 was distributed over a greater number of kilowatt-hours in the second case:

$4.00 ÷ 800 kwhr = $0.0050 or 0.5¢
$4.00 ÷ 1,600 kwhr = $0.0025 or 0.25¢
Difference 0.25¢

Going one step further, if we consider a customer who doubles his use of energy from 800 kwhr to 1,600 kwhr per month, but *does not* double his demand, the average cost per kwhr is altered materially.

Assume that the customer increased his demand only 50%, raising it from 3 kw (at 800 kwhr) to 4.5 kw (at 1,600 kwhr) per month, the unit cost would be as follows:

Demand Cost:	4.5 kw × $8.00	$36.00
Energy Cost:	1,600 kwhr × $0.04	64.00
Customer Cost:	1 customer × $4.00	4.00
Total Cost:		$104.00

Average cost per
kilowatt-hour: $104.00 ÷ 1,600 kwhr = $0.065 or 6.5¢

At 1,600 kwhr per month, the average cost per kwhr decreases from 7.25¢ to 6.5¢ per month when the load factor increases from 36.5% (at 6 kw) to 48.7% (at 4.5 kw), with no change in energy consumption (1,600 kwhr).

If we consider a much smaller customer, say one that uses only 50 kwhr per month, the customer cost has a much more pronounced effect on the average cost:

$4.00 \div 50 \text{ kwhr} = \$0.08$

If the load factor was the same as before the average rate for the 50 kwhr user would become:

(demand energy)   (customer)
    7.0¢   +   8.0¢   = 15¢ per kwhr

Recovery of the customer cost from small consumption customers may be made by embedding that cost in the early blocks of the schedule, thus injecting a declining price pattern in the rate as consumption increases.

It can also be handled by including a "customer" or "service" charge as a separate provision in the schedule.

Since each of the three cost components enters into the arithmetic of cost computation, it would seem logical that electric rates should be structured in three parts accordingly. In the past, this has been done to a limited degree, but many other factors have kept most rates stated in terms of one or two of the three components considered separately, but with the other costs embedded in them on an average basis in some manner.

Metering requirements

To determine the necessary parameters for billing these cost components, a primary consideration is the question of what type of meters should be installed—a simple kilowatt-hour meter for residential use or elaborate metering devices for large loads.

If, in addition to measuring the kilowatt-hours, provision is also to be made for measurement of the kilowatts of load, the additional investment in meters may not be justified. This is particularly true for residential service and for service to small commercial customers. Consequently, as a general rule, the installation of "demand meters" to measure the kilowatt level is usually confined to large commercial and industrial customers, and rate schedules for such consumers make separate provision for demand and energy related charges.

Residential rate schedules are generally the simplest rates in the utility tariff; they are usually based on energy measurement only and are flat or decrease the price per kilowatt-hour as the level of consumption increases. This "declining block" pattern follows the trend of cost which usually declines as volume goes up.

In special cases, such as street lighting, where the wattage of the lamps and the number of burning hours is known, the energy consumption may be computed arithmetically and no metering of the service is necessary.

RATE SCHEDULE DEVELOPMENT

From costs to rates

In the preceding chapters, we have noted the unique characteristics of this industry and examined certain costing methods used to support establishment of tariffs for the sale of electricity. The next logical step is to study the transition from these data to the formulation of the rate schedule itself using a hypothetical example.

Rates cannot be established individually for each customer, even though the cost of serving them may vary somewhat from one to the other. As a practical matter, they are developed for groups of customers such as residential, commercial, or industrial or for smaller groups, having generally similar patterns of use, within each group.

Illustrative rate schedules

The following three rate schedules represent simplified approaches to the problem of rate design. These are for example only and should not be applied to any individual company's rate design problem.

RATE A		
First	50 kwhr	16.0¢ kwhr
Next	50 kwhr	8.5¢ kwhr
Next	200 kwhr	7.5¢ kwhr
Next	500 kwhr	6.6¢ kwhr
Excess of	800 kwhr	6.0¢ kwhr

Minimum Bill $8.00 per month.

RATE B

First	50 kwhr	8.5¢ kwhr
Next	50 kwhr	8.0¢ kwhr
Next	200 kwhr	7.5¢ kwhr
Next	500 kwhr	6.5¢ kwhr
Excess of	800 kwhr	6.0¢ kwhr

Monthly Service Charge $4.00 per month.

RATE C

First	50 kwhr	10.0¢ per kwhr
Next	50 kwhr	6.0¢ per kwhr
Excess of	100 kwhr	4.0¢ per kwhr

All kw of Demand $4.00 per kilowatt at customer's meter. (Kilowatts of metered demand are assumed to equal twice the fully diversified kilowatts of class demand.)

Each of these rates would yield approximately $72,000,000 in annual revenue based on an assumed annual sales of one billion kilowatt-hours. (See Figures 6, 7, and 8.) A cost curve and other assumptions on which these schedules are based are developed later in this chapter.

Rate forms

Rates A, B and C generate approximately the *same* total system revenue under the assumed conditions. Rates A and B are simple kilowatt-hour rates containing five energy blocks. In Rate A, the customer cost component is embedded in the rate itself. In Rate B, the customer cost is recovered as a service charge independent of the energy charge provision.

Rate C is a two part rate schedule which incorporates customer cost in the energy charge, but makes a separate and independent charge for the demand cost component.

A single kilowatt-hour meter would be required for service under Schedules A or B. However, Schedule C requires that two measure-

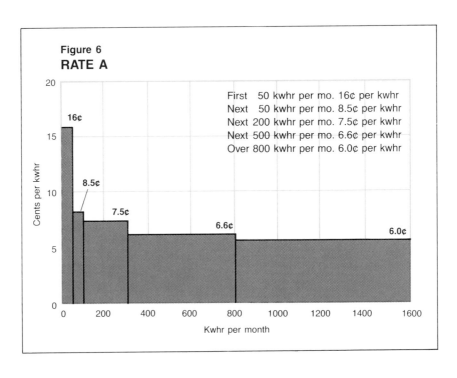

Figure 6
RATE A

First   50 kwhr per mo. 16¢ per kwhr
Next   50 kwhr per mo. 8.5¢ per kwhr
Next 200 kwhr per mo. 7.5¢ per kwhr
Next 500 kwhr per mo. 6.6¢ per kwhr
Over 800 kwhr per mo. 6.0¢ per kwhr

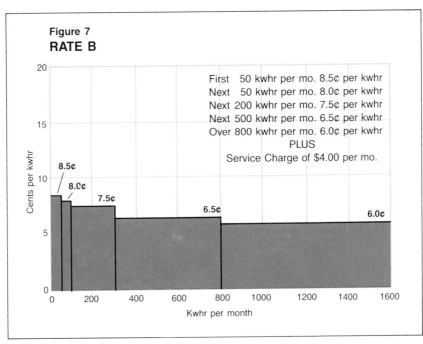

Figure 7
RATE B

First   50 kwhr per mo. 8.5¢ per kwhr
Next   50 kwhr per mo. 8.0¢ per kwhr
Next 200 kwhr per mo. 7.5¢ per kwhr
Next 500 kwhr per mo. 6.5¢ per kwhr
Over 800 kwhr per mo. 6.0¢ per kwhr
PLUS
Service Charge of $4.00 per mo.

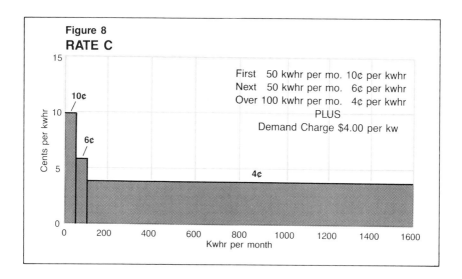

Figure 8
RATE C

First 50 kwhr per mo. 10¢ per kwhr
Next 50 kwhr per mo. 6¢ per kwhr
Over 100 kwhr per mo. 4¢ per kwhr
PLUS
Demand Charge $4.00 per kw

ments be made, since both kilowatt-hours and kilowatts would have to be recorded. This could be accomplished by installing a second meter to record the kilowatts of demand. However, it is usually done by install-ing a more complex instrument that serves both functions. By either method, the cost of metering for Schedule C would be considerably greater than that for either Schedule A or B.

Rates reflect average load factor

Under the block-energy rates form selected for A and B, the price assigned to each rate block can only be based on the *average load factor* at that level of consumption. This is predetermined by having com-bined the demand and energy cost components. Therefore, only one price can be quoted at any given level of consumption. However, that does not prevent the price set *at different consumption levels* from reflecting different load factors. Even so, the price stated at each level would still reflect only the average load characteristics of customers at that level of energy consumption.

An initial step in rate design procedure is to develop a "first trial" tariff that is reasonably simple in structure and is close to the pattern of cost throughout the expected range of energy consumption.

Relationship between load factor and coincidence of demand

The vital importance of load factor and of the coincidence of demand was discussed in the previous chapter and a hypothetical example was used to illustrate the effects. In that example, the demand at the generating station of 3 kilowatts was only one-half of the 6 kilowatt demand registered on the customer's meter at the point of delivery. These assumptions reflected a 50% coincidence factor attributable to the fact that each customer in the group did not make his maximum use of service at the same point in time.

The 6 kilowatt customer was assumed to have an energy consumption of 800 kilowatt-hours per month, and accordingly, a monthly load factor of 18.3%. However, other 6 kilowatt customers might operate at 10% load factor, a 30% load factor, or at some other level with energy consumptions commensurate with those characteristics.

Load research conducted over many years has indicated that, when large groups of customers are involved, there is a relationship between the average of individual load factors and the coincidence of demand. This is shown in the graph of Coincidence Factor vs Load Factor in Figure 9 (indicated as the C.F.–L.F. Curve). It is often called the Bary Curve in recognition of its originator, the late Constantine Bary, who was a pioneer in the field of load research.

Use of the C.F.–L.F. relationship in the determination of cost is illustrated by the several graphs in Figure 9 and the calculations shown in Table IV. Footnotes to the table describe the procedure which utilizes the C.F.–L.F. Curve to determine the appropriate Coincidence Factor, then applies that factor to the demand at the meter to calculate the coincident demand, and finally applies demand, energy and customer cost components to develop cost levels at the different monthly load factors involved.

Calculations are given in Table IV for the hypothetical case where the energy consumption is 800 kilowatt-hours per month, and the demand at the meter is 6 kilowatts thus reflecting a monthly load factor of 18.3%. Two additional points were computed for illustrative purposes, one at a load factor of 10% and the other at 30%. A greater number of points would be computed in actual practice to clearly define the cost curves.[1] Figure 9 shows the curve of total cost and also the curve of unit cost as determined by this procedure.

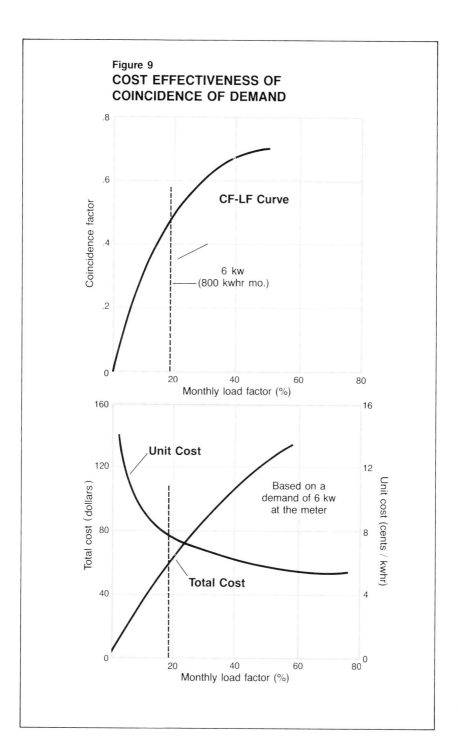

Figure 9
COST EFFECTIVENESS OF
COINCIDENCE OF DEMAND

CF-LF Curve

6 kw
(800 kwhr mo.)

Coincidence factor

Monthly load factor (%)

Unit Cost

Based on a
demand of 6 kw
at the meter

Total Cost

Total cost (dollars)

Unit cost (cents / kwhr)

Monthly load factor (%)

Table IV

COST CALCULATION AT DIFFERENT LEVELS OF COINCIDENT DEMAND

LOAD AND OPERATING CHARACTERISTICS

DEMAND (at meter)	6 kw	6 kw	6 kw
MONTHLY LOAD FACTOR	10%	18.3%	30%
ENERGY PER MONTH[1]	438 kwhr	800 kwhr	1314 kwhr
COINCIDENCE FACTOR[2]	.35	.50	.60
COINCIDENT DEMAND[3]	2.1 kw	3.0 kw	3.6 kw

COST COMPONENT APPLICATION

Customer	$4.00/bill	$ 4.00	$ 4.00	$ 4.00
Energy	$0.04/kwhr	17.52	32.00	52.56
Demand	$8.00/kw[4]	16.80	24.00	28.80
Total Cost		$38.32	$60.00	$85.36
Unit Cost per kwhr		8.75¢/kwhr	7.50¢/kwhr	6.50¢/kwhr

[1] Energy consumption is based on the assumed load factor and an average maximum demand at the customer's meter of 6 kw.

[2] Coincidence factor is determined from the Coincidence Factor-Load Factor Curve in the upper portion of Figure 9 entering the graph at the appropriate load factor and reading the coincidence factor on the vertical scale.

[3] Coincident demand is obtained by multiplying the kilowatts of demand at the meter by the coincidence factor obtained as indicated in footnote 2.

[4] Cost component of $8.00 is applicable to the coincident demand whereas the cost per kilowatt at the meter would be $4.00 for the hypothetical customer using 800 kwhrs per month and sustaining a 6 kw demand at the meter since under these conditions the coincidence factor would be .50 and the coincident demand would be 3 kw.

Compromise with cost

An important point, which the rate designer must constantly keep in mind, is the degree of compromise that any proposed tariff introduces in the cost-price relationship.

Rates A and B inherently introduce compromise with cost. Since these schedules do not contain a separate provision for a capacity or demand charge, cost can only be recovered on an average basis. The degree of compromise inherent in such rates depends on the range of differences in kilowatts of demand that exists among customers at each level of energy consumption.

Two part rate reduces compromise

Rate C introduces a separate charge for the demand, measured at the point of delivery, for each customer and thus eliminates the forced compromise aspect of the simpler schedules A and B. At the same time, it introduces a whole new aspect of ratemaking philosophy: placing an economic value on the kilowatt, not only on its magnitude, but also on its time of occurrence, in relation to the demands of other customers served by the utility. This is the most complex area with which rate designers must deal. It is also the most controversial and provokes the widest diversity of opinion on rate equitability.

Hopkinson rate form

The Rate C schedule, which sets forth separate charges for energy and demand, is termed a "Hopkinson" rate, named for its originator, Dr. John Hopkinson. An English engineer, he was a professor at Kings College, London, when he first proposed this type of tariff for electric service in 1897.

As shown by the examples previously discussed, different combinations of kilowatt-hours of energy, and kilowatts of demand, result in different levels of overall price per kilowatt-hour when the charges are combined. In other words, the average price paid under the rate varies with the load factor of the customer.

Wright rate form

The interrelationship of kilowatt-hours and kilowatts is directly reflected in a second basic rate form developed by another prominent

Englishman in 1896. Arthur Wright, an expert on utility finance, pointed out that the significant parameter on the pricing of electricity was the load factor and that its impact could be represented in a direct manner by calculating the simple arithmetic ratio of the kilowatt-hours of energy to the kilowatts of load. The price was quoted as *a unit cost per kilowatt-hour per kilowatt* during the billing period.

A rate of the form conceived by Arthur Wright, if derived from the Coincidence Factor-Load Factor and the Cost curves in Figure 10 might be the following:

First   20 kwhrs per kw of customer's demand ..... 15.0¢ kwhr
Next   20 kwhrs per kw .... 9.5¢ kwhr
Next   50 kwhrs per kw .... 6.0¢ kwhr
Next 100 kwhrs per kw .... 5.5¢ kwhr
Excess of 200 kwhrs per kw .... 5.0¢ kwhr

Modified Hopkinson rate form

It is said that many years later (1931), Mr. Wright asserted that Mr. Hopkinson's rate had achieved greater success. Just before his death, Wright graciously stated that "Wright was wrong and Hopkinson was right."

That statement, however, was premature because today many utilities have rate schedules which incorporate the basic features of both the Hopkinson and Wright rate forms. Energy charges are often quoted in terms of "kwhr per kw" or "hours use of the demand" and separate provisions are often made for a demand charge. Such rate schedules usually are applicable to commercial and industrial electric service and are termed "Modified Hopkinson Rates."

A modified rate might combine a separate demand charge such as the $4.00 per kilowatt for all kilowatts of demand as stated in the Hopkinson Schedule C. Added to that would be an energy charge based on the kilowatt-hours per kilowatt blocking of the Wright form of rate. It might provide a fixed energy block of a specific number of kilowatt-hours before expressing the rate in kilowatt-hours per kilowatt methodology. Many variations are used in order to adapt the rate to the specific load characteristics of the market served by a particular utility. Obviously, rates developed for one service area are not directly applicable to another. Modifications in rate form are usually indigenous to the service area involved.

Basis of illustrative rate examples

Specific assumptions on which the three illustrative rate examples are based embrace the following points:

1. Cost allocations have been made that assigned appropriate costs to the class of business for which the rate is to be designed.

2. Cost components have been developed for the demand, energy, and customers functions.

3. As the result of regulatory procedure, a total revenue target for the class has been established.

4. Complete records of prior sales of electricity are available in such form that total sales by rate blocks may be readily determined (both kwhr and kw).

5. Monthly load factor of customers using 50 kilowatt-hours per month was assumed to be 25 percent and load factor was presumed to increase with average customer size reaching 45% at a consumption level of 2,000 kilowatt-hours per month.

Based on these assumptions, an approximation of rate levels at different kilowatt-hour consumptions can be made by computing a cost curve such as that shown in Figure 10.

To develop such a relationship, the demand, energy, and customer cost components are applied using the load factor at each point throughout the range of the data.

Results for the hypothetical example are as follows:

At	50 kwhr	16.47¢ kwhr
	300 kwhr	9.11¢ kwhr
	800 kwhr	7.50¢ kwhr
	2,000 kwhr	6.64¢ kwhr

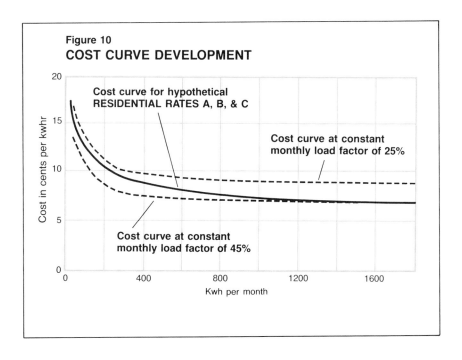

Figure 10
COST CURVE DEVELOPMENT

Cost curve for hypothetical
RESIDENTIAL RATES A, B, & C

Cost curve at constant
monthly load factor of 25%

Cost curve at constant
monthly load factor of 45%

In addition to the above values, Figure 10 also shows curves for constant load factors of 25% and 45%, the lowest and highest values assumed in the data. These curves bracket the cost curve as lower and upper limits.

Rate schedules were then developed which would result in bills approximating the values given on the cost curve throughout the range that the schedules were expected to cover. The block intervals and the block prices per kilowatt-hour are shown graphically and numerically in Figures 6, 7 and 8 for Rates A, B and C respectively.

An abbreviated comparison of cost curve values and bills is given below:

kwhr Per Mo.	Cost Curve Value	Bill Rate A	Bill Rate B	Bill Rate C
100	$ 12.21	$ 12.25	$ 12.25	$ 12.21
300	27.33	27.25	27.25	27.34
800	60.01	60.25	59.75	60.02
1000	71.74	72.25	71.75	71.74
2000	132.70	132.25	131.75	132.74

Significance of numbers

The rates developed as examples are expressed to a tenth of a cent for simplicity. If rates were expressed to smaller fractions of a cent, differences in bills under the different rates would be reduced. For example, in Schedule B, raising the fourth block rate from 6.5¢ to 6.55¢ would raise the bill for 800 kwhr from $59.75 to $60.00 thus conforming to the cost index.

Any change in block rate would have an effect on the total revenue produced by the schedule. Of the total energy sales of one billion kilowatt-hours per year assumed for the example, 360 million kilowatt-hours were sold in the fourth rate block. An increase in rate from 6.5¢ to 6.55¢, a change of five one-hundredths of one cent would increase the total revenue from the schedule by $180,000.

Rates are designed to approach the total revenue target as nearly as possible, but not to exceed it. Each step in rate design procedure must be checked for its impact on total revenue as well as for the impact on individual bills.

Computations of total revenue generated by Rates A and B are given in Table V. Computations for Rate C are given in Table VI.

Table V

DEVELOPMENT OF ANNUAL REVENUE UNDER RATES A AND B

	Annual kwhr	Unit Rate	Annual Revenue
RATE A			
First 50 kwhr/mo.	55,000,000	● 16.0¢	$ 8,800,000
Next 50 kwhr/mo.	55,000,000	8.5¢	4,675,000
Next 200 kwhr/mo.	210,000,000	7.5¢	15,750,000
Next 500 kwhr/mo.	360,000,000	6.6¢	23,760,000
Over 800 kwhr/mo.	320,000,000	6.0¢	19,200,000
RATE A	1,000,000,000 kwhr		$ 72,185,000[1]
RATE B			
First 50 kwhr/mo.	55,000,000	● 8.5¢	$ 4,675,000
Next 50 kwhr/mo.	55,000,000	8.0¢	4,400,000
Next 200 kwhr/mo.	210,000,000	7.5¢	15,750,000
Next 500 kwhr/mo.	360,000,000	6.5¢[2]	23,400,000
Over 800 kwhr/mo.	320,000,000	6.0¢	19,200,000
	1,000,000,000 kwhr		$ 67,425,000
Service Charge 100,000 customers × 12 months × $4.00 per bill ..			$ 4,800,000
RATE B			$ 72,225,000[1]

[1] In actual practice, rate schedules would be expressed with additional decimal places, and on that basis, would be designed so that the revenue difference between the two rates would not be significant.

[2] For example: If the rate applicable to the fourth block of Schedule B was expressed as 6.49¢ instead of 6.5¢, the difference between revenues produced by Schedules A and B would be only $4000 per year instead of $40,000 per year.

Table VI

DEVELOPMENT OF ANNUAL REVENUE UNDER RATE C

	Annual kwhr	Rate per Unit	Annual Revenue
ENERGY CHARGE			
First 50 kwhr/mo.	55,000,000	● 10¢	$ 5,500,000
Next 50 kwhr/mo.	55,000,000	● 6¢	3,300,000
Over 100 kwhr/mo.	890,000,000	● 4¢	35,600,000
	1,000,000,000 kwhr		$ 44,400,000
DEMAND CHARGE			
All kw's	6,950,000 kw-mos. @ 4.00		$ 27,800,000
TOTAL ANNUAL REVENUE FROM RATE C			$ 72,200,000

Footnote, Chapter 5

[1] In actual practice, all values of kilowatt-hours and kilowatts measured at the generating station would have to be adjusted to allow for line and other losses between the point of production and the point of delivery. Such adjustments were omitted for purposes of simplification.

TIME-OF-USE RATES

Cost varies with time of use

It is inherent in the physical process of generating electricity and delivering it to the consumer that the cost of production varies with the time of day and the season of the year. This arises from the need to meet different levels of load on the system with different types of generating equipment as was discussed in Chapter 1. It was pointed out that various combinations of base load, cycling, and peaking units are required, depending on the magnitude of the load in kilowatts and the duration of the load being supplied. Since each type of equipment is designed for a different purpose, the technical characteristics of each type are different, as are both the capital investment per kilowatt and the operating expense per kilowatt-hour. The average system cost of power is a complex mixture of these ingredients.

Theoretically, it may be said that the unit cost of production varies from minute to minute. However, such changes are relatively small, and practical ratemaking considers these effects over a longer interval of time, such as a half-hour or an hour. Even on this longer basis, the hour-to-hour changes in cost are still not very significant during those periods when system load is relatively constant. It is when major changes in load level take place such as from midafternoon to 3:00 a.m. that the difference in unit cost becomes significant in terms of rate design.

Time of day vs. season of the year

Many references are made to time-of-day rates to indicate those that change the pricing level between day and night hours. A more general description is implied by time-of-use rates which reflect pricing differences during different seasons of the year, as well as the nighttime to daytime changes. Popular usage has made the terms appear to be synonymous, although that is not technically correct.

All electric rates must consider the time of use of the service as well as the maximum load in kilowatts, and the energy requirement in kilowatt-hours; the mechanism for accomplishing this objective varies widely. The direct approach is to use metering equipment that will record each of the quantities independently. However, rates which make no provision whatsoever for time-of-use measurement may nevertheless give indirect consideration to the time factor.

Influence of weather

Seasonal patterns may give indirect time-of-day measurement. For example, if electricity for space-heating is furnished through a separate meter and no other load is connected to it, the time of use of service is largely determined by the weather. Greatest use of service usually occurs during the coldest hours of the day, from midnight to dawn. Although the requirements change on days of different minimum temperature, the overall seasonal pattern repeats itself with remarkable regularity. Weather is the principal determining factor; and since the time of use is known by indirect inference, the price can be established appropriately without actual time measurement.

Indirect time-of-use considerations

Another form of indirect time-of-use consideration can be a residential block-energy rate, with a trailing block which begins at a point where typical kilowatt-hour usage for the essential domestic needs has been already covered. Additional usage would be assumed to be from some special application such as water-heating or space-heating. Since such an approach is based on assumed levels of basic use which are not the same as the actual usage by each consumer, it cannot be a precise approach. Its recognition of time-of-use follows from the assumption that energy required above the essential level is incremental and probably off-peak in nature—as, for example, space-heating for a summer peaking utility.

Consider a rate schedule which contains a demand charge based on the maximum demand of the customer during the billing period. Even without limiting its application to a specific time of day, the rate schedule still has a time-of-use inference. Since the charge is based only on the individual customer's maximum demand, he can materially reduce his bill by shifting some of his usage to different hours of the day. He can continue to do so until his demand at the new peak load time is equal to the load that remains on the line at his original peak period.

Flexibility of approach

There are many ways in which the time element is considered in addition to the direct approach of actually measuring it. In the previous chapter, sample Rates A, B, and C were purposely designed to be as simple as possible for illustration purposes. No seasonal or nighttime variation in rate level was considered nor was any specific final application of electricity specified.

Rate design must recognize market characteristics of the service area involved. It is the simultaneous use of service by its customers, in aggregate, that establishes the utility's system peak, and thus is the most substantial factor, in most instances, in setting its need for capital.

Variations in the cost of producing electricity are directly related to the load and its fluctuations, and consequently reflect the way in which the consumer uses the service. The pattern of daily variation or diurnal cycle in the use of electricity naturally reflects the living habits of inhabitants of the service area involved. In almost every instance, the demand for power during daytime hours exceeds usage at nighttime by a substantial margin.

In addition, most utilities experience substantial differences in demand for electricity during different seasons of the year. These seasonal cycles arise from the varying hours of daylight, temperature, and other climatic conditions, as well as from noncontinuous occupancies as are often characteristic of vacation and resort areas. Large industrial loads can materially affect the overall pattern.

Effect of large specific loads

Very large specific loads, such as air conditioning in summer months, and electric space-heating in winter, can have a determining influence on whether the utility has a summer peak, a winter peak, or a seasonally-balanced load. Winter peaks are usually sustained in December during late afternoon or early evening hours when space-heating is not involved. Space-heating tends to peak in the early hours just before sunrise on cold winter days. Air conditioning peaks on the utility system are sustained in early afternoon hours during the hottest part of the summer day. The air conditioning peak demand usually occurs in July, August, or September depending on geographic location.

Rates for seasonal variation

Reflecting the seasonal variation in load can be accomplished easily by stipulating higher prices for electric service during the probable peak months than during other months. If this procedure is followed, no change in metering equipment is necessary. Many utilities have rates based on this principle, especially where there is a high saturation of air conditioning.

Rates for day-night variation

In contrast to the rate design procedure for the seasonal cycle, monitoring the diurnal cycle is more complex. In addition to measuring the number of kilowatt-hours delivered to the consumer, provision can also be made to measure his demand in kilowatts or, if this is not done, to record the kilowatt-hours used during the peak hours of the day independently of those delivered during other hours. The demand costs are then recovered on an average basis through the medium of the energy charge.

Direct measurement of demand may be made in a number of ways. A separate meter may be installed that measures demand, or a special meter may be used that combines both kinds of measurement in a single instrument.

Separate records of kilowatt-hours used during peak hours and other hours of the day may be made by installing a second kilowatt-hour meter and an automatic switching device to transfer from one meter to the other at the proper time or through the use of some other device.

Regardless of which approach is taken, the additional metering costs involved in establishing a rate which is dependent on the time of use of service are significant. Accordingly, a careful economic analysis must be made to determine whether the additional investment is justified for the particular group of customers under consideration.

Broadly speaking, time-of-use rate design has been directed toward large-use customers. This has been done not only because of equipment cost considerations, but also because large customers, by their very nature, have a greater potential for energy conservation, and for shifting load from on-peak hours to other periods of the day.

Example of time-of-use rate

A simplified time-of-use rate for residential service is illustrated by Rate D, shown below, an example using only the basic concepts of this form of rate design. At the prices stated, Rate D would produce approximately the same total revenue as would Rates A, B and C.

RATE D

	On-Peak* Hours	Off-Peak Hours
SUMMER MONTHS		
Demand Charge	$7.00/kw	$2.00/kw
Energy Charge	4.25¢/kwhr	4.00¢/kwhr
WINTER MONTHS		
Demand Charge	$3.50/kw	$2.00/kw
Energy Charge	3.25¢/kwhr	2.50¢/kwhr
CUSTOMER SERVICE CHARGE	$4.00 per Month	

*On-peak hours are assumed to be 10:00 a.m. to 10:00 p.m.

Although this illustrative rate depicts the fundamentals of the time-of-use tariff, there are a great many possible variations of this basic theme—some simpler and some considerably more complex.

Determination of rating periods

The time intervals used in designing time-of-use rate levels are called rating periods. These are usually described as on-peak, intermediate (or shoulder), and off-peak. Although the cost of production does vary continuously, it would be highly impractical to set a different price for each of the hours of the day, for 365 days a year. Dividing the day into two or three costing periods represents a reasonable compromise in most cases.

The number of rating periods selected, the length of these periods, and such seasonal modifications as may be necessary, are dependent on the nature of the aggregate load served by the utility and the schedule of operations of the generating units used to supply it. A study of the utility's mix of base load, cycling, and peaking units is the beginning point, since it is the particular mix of such units that are in operation at any specific time that determines the cost of production of that time.

Meeting seasonal load patterns

System load curves for different seasons of the year are developed and compared with corresponding load curves for prior years. The objective is to determine the repeated patterns of load level and load change that are characteristic of each season. The stability of these curves, or in other words, the degree to which the same pattern repeats in successive years is of prime importance if a rate is to be based on these seasonal relationships.

Assume that the utility has a summer peak that is substantially greater than the peak load served in winter. Loads during spring and fall seasons would be at levels between the summer and winter peak values. (See Figures 11, 12, 13 and 14.)

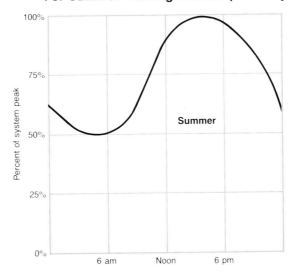

Figure 11
SEASONAL SYSTEM LOADS
For Summer-Peaking Utilities (Weekdays)

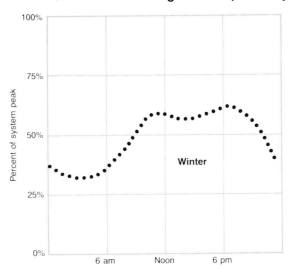

Figure 12
SEASONAL SYSTEM LOADS
For Summer-Peaking Utilities (Weekdays)

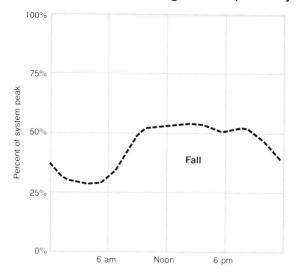

Figure 13
SEASONAL SYSTEM LOADS
For Summer-Peaking Utilities (Weekdays)

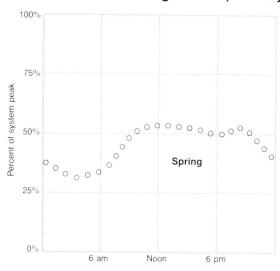

Figure 14
SEASONAL SYSTEM LOADS
For Summer-Peaking Utilities (Weekdays)

Base load, cycling & peaking units

The summer peak load, in this example, would be met by a combination of generating units. For purposes of illustration, assume that the
generating equipment needed to supply the system peak is as follows:

Peaking Units	10%
Cycling Units	30%
Base Load Units	60%
Total	100%

Use of peaking units

Peaking units are least expensive from the capital investment point of
view but the most expensive from the viewpoint of operating expense.
Designed to operate for only a relatively few hours per year, possibly
400 to 800, they are flexible enough to bring on line quickly. They are
an optimal economic choice for the utility to use on those few days
when peak loads occur.

Figure 15 shows the generation pattern used by the utility to meet
the system summer peak day load. A line across the chart at 90% of the
peak load (10% below the peak demand) indicates that the peaking
units would be required from about 12:00 noon to 8:00 p.m. At other
hours, the load could be carried by the cycling and base load generating
equipment.

Use of base load & cycling units

A line across the chart at 60% of the peak demand indicates that all
load below that level could be carried by the base load units and that
more capacity would be needed during the period extending from 8:00
a.m. to midnight. This capacity would come from the cycling units,
except for that portion supplied by peaking units.

Final selection of rating periods

Based on these observations, the 24 hours of the peak day might be

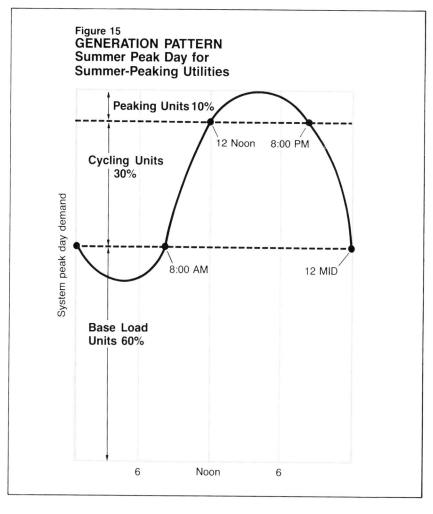

Figure 15
GENERATION PATTERN
Summer Peak Day for
Summer-Peaking Utilities

divided into three rating periods, on-peak, off-peak and intermediate.

An on-peak period would be established representing that portion of the day during which all categories of generating equipment would be required to meet the load. These hours would extend from 12:00 noon to 8:00 p.m. and would be the hours of highest production cost.

The off-peak period would represent those hours during which only base load units would be needed to carry the load. As shown on the chart, these would extend from 12:00 midnight until 8:00 a.m.

During hours other than those selected for the on-peak and off-peak periods, a combination of cycling and base load units would be required. Again, as indicated on the chart, this would occur at two different times of the day, first between 8:00 a.m. and 12:00 noon, and then again between 8:00 p.m. and 12:00 midnight. Such intervals are designated as intermediate periods.

Summarizing these rating periods' limits, the three divisions of the day would be as follows:

On-Peak   - 12:00 noon to 8:00 p.m.

Intermediate - 8:00 a.m. to 12:00 noon and 8:00 p.m. to 12:00 midnight

Off-Peak   - 12:00 midnight to 8:00 a.m.

Economics of generating units

Base load generating equipment requires the greatest capital investment per kilowatt, but has the lowest operating expense, just the opposite of the characteristics of the peaking units. The economics of cycling units usually falls somewhere between the two. Because of these basic cost characteristics, it generally follows that the average cost of electricity is greatest during on-peak hours, in middle range during the intermediate period, and lowest during the off-peak period. The degree of difference will vary greatly from one utility to another depending on the specific load characteristics of its service area and the economics of the region that it services.

Summer vs. winter rating periods

The tentative selection of rating periods established by analysis of the summer load may be changed when a similar study is made of the load patterns during other seasons of the year.

Figure 16 shows the winter load curve of the same hypothetical utility. Since the summer load in this example was assumed to be much greater than the winter load, the utility's plant investment is based on meeting its summer peak.

It follows that base load equipment will handle a greater percentage of the winter peak since that peak is well below the summer level. If we assume that 85% of winter peak can be carried by base load generating

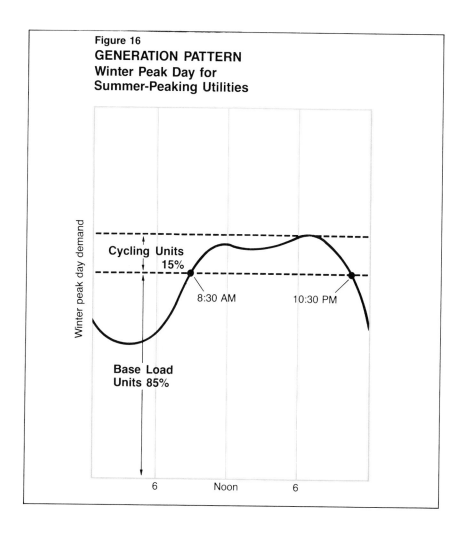

Figure 16
GENERATION PATTERN
Winter Peak Day for
Summer-Peaking Utilities

units, a line across the chart at the 85% level indicates that additional capacity would be needed during the interval from 8:30 a.m. to 10:30 p.m. Note that this period corresponds closely to the 8:00 a.m. and 12:00 midnight points selected for the summer period. However, since only 15% more capacity is needed than that which can be supplied by the base load units, there would be no need to draw upon the peaking units at all during the winter.

Professional judgment required

As a practical matter, the determination of rating periods for time-of-use rate design must involve a great deal of professional judgment. Analyses, such as those just discussed, offer substantial guidance in the design process, but decisions must be made on the basis of many additional factors.

For example, a decision must be made as to the number of rating periods used. Most time-of-use rates are based on dividing the day into two or three intervals, although there is no theoretical reason why a greater number might not be employed. It is largely a matter of administrative practicability.

Rating periods selected for one season of the year may not be applicable to another without modification or deletion. In most cases, Saturdays, Sundays, and holidays will be priced independently at lower rates because of the reduced use of electricity on those days.

Two basic objectives

Time-of-use rates have two major objectives. One goal is to have a closer correlation between cost and price for the individual consumer than is possible with tariffs that do not consider time of use. A second aim is to encourage conservation, and to induce customers to make changes in their patterns of use that improve the overall load pattern, and reduce the peak load for a given output of energy.

Shifting of load from on-peak to off-peak periods would not only be beneficial to the customers involved, but would inure to the benefit of other customers by improving the load factor of the class of business as a whole. The consequent reduction in peak would reduce the need to install additional high-cost generating units.

Aside from the mechanical problems and costing procedures of time-of-use rate design, close attention must be given to the incentive effects of the price levels established so that the load shifting and conservation impact will be retained on the final design. It is not always possible to inject the designed incentive into a rate without dropping the price below actual cost. For example, if electricity is used in some specialized manufacturing process, no amount of price reduction in electric service would serve as an incentive if the manufacturer can use an alternative fuel to do the same job at a lower price.

Customer response to rate design

The degree to which a customer responds to a change in price is price elasticity. It is simply a measure of how much less of a product the consumer uses when the price is increased and how much more will be used if the price drops. Electricity for essential purposes in the home is considered to be basically "inelastic" or, in other words, not affected by price change very much. However, electricity for nonessential applications, once the essential uses are taken care of, does have significant price elasticity, the degree of which will depend on the particular end use of service involved. Customers will rarely cut off refrigerators to save money, but they may dispense with air conditioning on the milder days of the summer to economize. Price elasticity in electric service is difficult to measure although much investigative work has been done in this field.

In regulatory practice, it is recognized that price elasticity is present. However, the inability to measure it precisely makes it difficult to estimate conservation of energy, shifting of load, and any change in utility revenue which might take place after time-of-use rates have been put in effect. It is a problem for regulators and for regulated utilities alike, and is the subject of considerable research effort today.

Peak load pricing connotations

Peak load pricing is often used in discussions of time-of-use rate design, sometimes in a synonymous sense. Peak load pricing, first of all, describes the basic concept of central station utility service. The cost of service is primarily dependent on the commitment that the utility must make to supply that peak.

The term underscores the economic importance of the peak requirement concept whether it is at the system level, the class of business level, or at the level of the individual consumer. At each level, the peak load requirement is a governing factor, and its overall impact is a function of the time at which it occurs. Diversity of load occurrence, as previously noted, is the all-important element in the economic base on which utility rate design rests.

LOAD RESEARCH

The need for knowledge

Although load research is a complex engineering-statistical discipline, it can be described in simpler terms: it is simply a method of learning more about the way in which consumers use the service that the utility provides.

Kilowatt-hours and kilowatts, load factor, and time of use have been defined and discussed repeatedly in earlier chapters because they are the principal dimensions of the product which the utility furnishes. One must know the size of the load in numerical terms in order to design and operate the electric system and, finally, to provide the rate designer with the information needed to put the price on the utility's product.

Load requirements

The power company supplies service to all of its customers who want service at any given time. Therefore, the system's load is a mixture of many different patterns of use. Some groups of customers have similar characteristics; others do not. The aggregate requirement reflects the dimensions established by thousands or millions of consumers.

As discussed earlier, customers may be divided for load research purposes into three major categories:

Residential
Small Commercial
Large Commercial

Class load requirements

Within each of these groups, there is a trended similarity in use pattern throughout the range from smallest to largest user. However, between the categories, the basic load patterns are relatively dissimilar, and it is for this reason that separate rate schedules are appropriate.

The utility must determine not only the patterns of use of individual customers but also the combined pattern of use of all customers on an hour-to-hour basis. It must measure interaction between the individual consumers, and evaluate the diversity existing between them because of differences in time of maximum use of service.

Regular load research programs

It is not economically feasible to install special metering equipment for load research purposes at every customer location. Instead, such measurements are made on a statistical sample of representative consumers.

Extensive load testing is usually carried out on classes of business such as residential and commercial. For most utilities, the number of customers in these groups is in the thousands. In contrast, an industrial group might be composed of only a few hundred users. Utilities are increasingly adopting regular load research programs, alternately checking residential and commercial class loads on a repetitive basis and other special categories as needed.

Periodic class tests

Ideally, all classes of business should be load-tested at the same time. However, this requires a great many special meters and is very expensive in terms of capital investment and processing costs. Since class load characteristics do not change rapidly from year to year, the additional cost of simultaneous testing of all classes may not justify the additional expense.

Load research is an expensive undertaking. Statistical accuracy may

Table VII
SAMPLING GROUP LIMITS FOR RESIDENTIAL LOAD RESEARCH TESTS

GROUP	I	0 to 100	kilowatt-hours per month
GROUP	II	101 to 250	kilowatt-hours per month
GROUP	III	251 to 500	kilowatt-hours per month
GROUP	IV	501 to 800	kilowatt-hours per month
GROUP	V	801 to 1200	kilowatt-hours per month
GROUP	VI	1201 to 1800	kilowatt-hours per month
GROUP	VII	1801 to 2500	kilowatt-hours per month
GROUP	VIII	2501 to 3500	kilowatt-hours per month
GROUP	IX	3501 to 5000	kilowatt-hours per month
GROUP	X	5001 and over	kilowatt-hours per month

Note: The number of test groups in the sample and the specific limits selected for each group will depend upon the individual utility's statistical distribution of customers by size and upon the statistical accuracy required.

require a sample of 500 customers for a single class load test that would normally be conducted for a year or longer. The installed cost of the special metering equipment is around $1,000 per installation and, in addition to the fixed charges, there are substantial operating expenses for data collection, computer processing and technical analysis.

Hypothetical example—assumptions

In recent years, technological progress in load research has advanced at an extremely rapid pace. As a consequence, today's techniques are highly complex electrically and very sophisticated in terms of data processing methods. Despite this complexity, in practice, the basic measurement on which all such programs are based is simple in concept. The following hypothetical example sets forth the principle. Assume that:

1. A sample of 500 customers has been selected by statistical methods to represent the residential class of customers served by the utility.

2. Within that sample, ten subgroups have been determined to represent customers of increasing size, from the smallest to the largest,

with 50 sample customers in each subgroup in the arrangement shown in Table VII.

3. Meters are installed at each customer location to measure the kilo-watt-hour consumption and to make a continuous record of the kilowatt demand of that customer.

4. The test runs for at least one year.

Load testing objectives

The objectives of the load research program are to obtain the following:

1. A record of kilowatt-hour consumption by billing months and by rating periods within the billing month, in some cases.

2. An hour-to-hour record of the variation in each customer's load.

3. The maximum kilowatt demand established by each customer.

4. The maximum kilowatt demand established by customers during certain periods of particular technical interest, as during system peak hours of the day or season of the year.

5. The maximum demand established simultaneously by all of the customers in each group at whatever time that may occur.

6. The maximum demand established simultaneously by all of the customers in each group during certain periods of particular technical interest.

Values to be derived from test data

In addition to the direct measurements of kilowatt-hours and kilowatts, other significant values are computed from the results. Some of these values are as follows:

1. The relationship is ascertained between the maximum kilowatt demand established simultaneously by all customers and the arithmetic sum of the maximum demands of the individual customers

regardless of the time at which they occur. (This relationship is termed the coincident factor and is often said to be the most important of all of the load research results.) The term "diversity factor" refers to the same relationship, but in reciprocal arithmetic form:

$$D.F. = \frac{1}{C.F.}$$

2. The diversity coincidence relationships are obtained between the sample groups of customers similar to the determination in item one for such ratios within each group.

The basic steps of the method used in this example are shown in Table VIII.

Basic computer tabulation

It is important to recognize the volume of numerical work involved in load research. If demands are recorded for each half-hour interval, 48 readings would be recorded for each customer being studied on a daily basis. For a group of 50 customers, a typical sample group, this becomes 2,400 entries per day; 72,000 for a 30-day month; and 876,000 entries for a one-year test period. For a residential class load study comprised of ten such test groups, the one-year requirement for basic data would mean that 8,760,000 entries of demand data would have to be made. Although load research has been carried on by utilities for many years, it is only the full application of computer processing that has made it possible to handle this enormous volume of information.

Details of tabular values

So much for the primary record of test results. What is done with all of this information? Table VIII, and the graph included in it, illustrates the basic principle involved.

Table VIII illustrates a section of the daily data sheet for the afternoon and evening hours from 3:00 p.m. to 9:00 p.m. Hypothetical de-

Table VIII

EXAMPLE OF TABULATION OF INDIVIDUAL CUSTOMER DEMANDS (kw) DETERMINED FROM LOAD RESEARCH TESTS

Test Customer Number	P.M. 3:00	3:30	4:00	4:30	5:00	5:30	6:00	6:30	7:00	7:30	8:00	8:30	9:00
1.	1.90	1.70	1.60	1.60	1.60	1.60	1.50	1.50	1.60	2.40	3.20	*4.00*	*4.00*
2.	1.30	1.20	1.25	1.20	1.15	1.20	1.65	2.20	*2.40*	2.20	2.15	2.20	2.20
3.	1.00	1.05	1.05	1.00	*3.00*	1.15	1.20	1.20	1.20	1.15	1.25	1.20	1.10
AVE	1.40	1.32	1.30	1.27	1.93	1.32	1.45	1.63	1.73	1.02	2.20	*2.46*	2.43

mand values in kilowatts have been estimated for 3 of the 50 test customers involved. These numbers, somewhat exaggerated for the purposes of illustration, have been averaged for each half-hour interval depicted. The purpose of the graphic display is to illustrate the manner in which these customers' requirements for electric service would be met if those requirements were consolidated.

Intragroup values

Referring to the chart, the peak demand for each of the three customers occurs at a different hour of the day. Customer #1 peaks at 8:30 p.m., customer #2 at 7:00 p.m., customer #3 at 5:00 p.m. Their maximum demands for the day were 4.0 kw, 2.4 kw, and 3.0 kw, respectively.

Individual customer demands were added-up for each half-hour period as shown in the tabulation on the top of Table VIII. For example, customers #1, #2, and #3 had respective demands of 1.90 kw, 1.30 kw, and 1.00 kw, which totalled 4.20 kw. When divided by three, the average demand per customer becomes 1.40 kw for the half-hour ending at 3:00 p.m. Average demands similarly computed for other half-hour periods were developed, and the maximum value for the three cases, in aggregate, was 2.46 kw, which occured at 8:30 p.m. A plot of the combined values is shown by the heavy black line on the chart.

The significant result of this procedure is that the simultaneous demand of the three customers together occured at 8:30 p.m. and was 7.40 kilowatts, which was less than the sum of the three individual customer maximum demands.

If we consider the maximum demands of each without regard to time of occurrence, the totals is 9.4 kw (4.0 kw + 2.4 kw + 3.0 kw) or an equivalent of 3.13 kw each.

However, the maximum simultaneous demand of the three customers together, as previously noted, was only 2.46 kw per customer or only 79% of the nonsimultaneous equivalent of 3.13 kw.

The importance of this relationship cannot be over-emphasized because the utility's investment in generating equipment must be planned to meet the simultaneous or coincident maximum demand of all its customers. As has been noted, if it were not for differences in time of maximum use among customers, the cost of electricity to the customer would easily be twice as great as it actually is today.

In the case of the three customers just discussed, the two parameters that are germane to the time-of-use concept are the following:

$$\text{Coincidence Factor} = \frac{\text{Coincident Max. kw}}{\text{Non-Coincident Max. kw}} = \frac{2.46}{3.13} = 0.79$$

$$\text{Diversity Factor} = \frac{\text{Non-Coincident Max. kw}}{\text{Coincident Max. kw}} = \frac{3.13}{2.46} = 1.27$$

Using only three customers and limiting the time to a single day simplifies the problem for purposes of illustration. However, in actuality, whenever 50 test customers are involved and a test period extending over several months or years is analyzed, the numerical value of the coincidence and diversity factors would probably be quite different. On a day other than that used for the example, the demands of the three customers might exceed those in the example, and the demands of the additional 47 customers could materially change the final results.

Intergroup values

Having determined the maximum coincident demand in kilowatts of a 50-customer test group, the way in which that pattern combines with those of the other nine test groups must be explored. This would be done in the same way as was done with the individual customers—evaluating one test group against another. However, since the 50 test customers in one group may not represent the same percentage of all customers in its consumption (kwhr) band as does another group, an additional factor must be considered. An adjustment for weighting, based on the original sampling procedure, must be made before the coincidence between groups is computed.

Synthesis of class load curves

The coincidence relationship between individual customers in a test group is usually termed the *Intragroup* Coincidence Factor, and the relationship between the test groups is called the *Intergroup* Coincidence Factor.

When all of the intragroup and intergroup values have been determined, the demand data in kilowatts may be used to synthesize a class load curve representing all of the customers in the class of business involved. This class load pattern becomes the foundation for the allocation of costs discussed in previous chapters (Chapters 4 and 5).

In classes of business such as large commercial and industrial, meters already being installed for billing purposes may furnish some of the research data directly. If that is the case, this data must be statistically combined with data developed from special meters installed specifically for load research purposes.

LOAD MANAGEMENT

Sources of efficiency improvement

Any significant improvement in the overall functioning of the electric utility usually comes from one of two sources. First, operating costs may be reduced either by administrative action or by increased technical efficiency of equipment. Second, an improvement in the load characteristics of customers served by the utility can provide a fundamental change by which both administrative actions and system designs may materially benefit.

Cost reduction by management decision is initiated by the utility. Cost benefits arising from improvement in load characteristics, while originating on the customers' premises, are a joint venture of the customer and the utility. They may result from the installation of load limiting devices, from deliberate changes in customer operating procedure, and from the effect of load improvement incentives built into the utility's rate structure. The interest in time-of-use pricing is directed toward load factor improvement by reduction in peak demand.

Load factor improvement—two ways

It is important to note that load factor improvement (increase) may be accomplished in two ways which are quite different in their economic impact.

System peak demand may be reduced without a corresponding change in the number of kilowatt-hours of energy delivered. Changes of this nature take place if a customer reduces his demand or continues the same activities, but can change the time of day or season of the year at which some operations are carried out. If an operation can be shifted away from the peak time, the aggregate demand of all consumers is reduced even though the same total activities are not affected. Time of use is the key concept for this kind of change, and the ultimate result is a reduction in investment in plant and other equipment.

The second method of improving load factor would be to increase the kilowatt-hours of energy delivered with no corresponding change in the system peak demand. Changes of this nature result from making greater use of facilities already installed or, in other words, an increase in use during off-peak times. This kind of change does not reduce the investment in plant but permits the sale of additional kilowatt-hours at a cost corresponding largely to the incremental cost of fuel.

While the utility has no direct control over the patterns of use of service by its customers, it can offer rate structure incentives for improvement.

Effect of off-peak rates

Throughout the history of the industry, many utilities have offered lower rates for service delivered during off-peak hours when generating plants are not operating at full capacity. One of the most common applications has been an off-peak rate for electric water heating. Under such a tariff, electricity for that purpose is supplied through a separate meter and is available only during the specific hours set forth in the rate. A clock-controlled switch or other timing device automatically disconnects the water heater at other times of the day. The heater is selected with the necessary water capacity and thermal insulation so that an adequate supply of hot water is stored during the hours of nonoperation.

Incentives for load shifting

The off-peak rate for water heating is different from a time-of-use rate. Both offer a lower price for off-peak service, but the time-of-use anticipates that the price incentive will persuade consumers to shift some load from the on-peak to off-peak periods.

Controlled water heating envisions a predetermined fixed pattern of usage. A time-of-use rate, on the other hand, while employing the same pricing mechanism, is intended to change the pattern of some use and thereby improve the overall load characteristics of the system.

With the dramatic increases in cost of fuel in recent years, customers have been greatly concerned about the rapidly increasing cost of electricity. Customers may control their loads and minimize bills either by reducing their use of service or by shifting the time at which electricity is used for some applications in order to conserve energy.

Except for a reduction in total energy consumption, control of load involves management of the demand sustained (kilowatts) in both magnitude and timing. In order to do this effectively, the consumer would need to monitor the demand he is imposing on the system at all times. Since it would not be practical to have someone continuously watch a demand meter, mechanical or electrical means are useful.

Interlocking devices

A device which interlocks large appliances provides a simple mechanical means for controlling load in a residence. Such a device might interlock an electric range and electric water heater, so that only one may operate at the same time. The range would be given priority so that, when it was turned on, the water heater could not come on the line at the same time. If the water heater was already in operation when the range was turned on, the water heater would be turned off until the range was no longer in use—or at least for some predetermined period of time. Since the water heater is inherently a storage device, enough hot water would be available to carry over during the relatively short period of time required for cooking.

Interlocking, as this process is called, can be done in a great many different ways and may involve almost any kind of large-use electrical equipment.

Interruption of service

Interrupting the use of service to customers' appliances on a random, individual basis can reduce the overall system demand by creating an artificial diversity in time of use. While it is necessary for heating or cooling devices to catch up when service is resupplied, the advantage is that all customers do not make up their deficiency at exactly the same instant. Experiments are being conducted by many utilities using the "random interrupting" technique to reduce the air-conditioning system demand in residential service.

Alerting signals

There are some devices that may help a customer reduce his load. The simplest are warning lights or audible buzzers that alert a customer that his load level has reached a predetermined point. Armed with this information, he can reduce his demand in the interest of keeping his bill down.

More sophisticated devices that alert the customer when the set level is reached and, in addition, automatically turn off some electrical equipment are also available. When time-of-day rates are in effect, the device could be used to alert the customer that higher priced on-peak hours are approaching.

Load anticipating devices

Figure 17 illustrates some principles of load management. Item 2 is the customer's load curve on a day of normal load pattern. This curve reaches a peak value, Reference 1, at 6:30 p.m., and it is assumed that this peak value of the customer's demand would be used in the computation of his electric bill. The anticipated level of the peak demand would be predetermined by reviewing the actual values established by the consumer in prior billing months. It becomes a target value that should not be exceeded in the interest of keeping future bills as low as possible.

Reference 3 shows the curve on a day of unusually high load level, and Reference 6 shows the curve on a day of low load level. Either curve might develop on a given day, but the customer would not normally know in advance which curve it might be. Therefore, to avoid exceeding the previous billing peak, it is necessary to monitor the rate

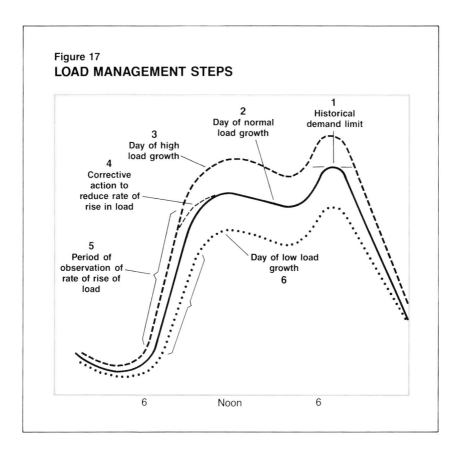

Figure 17
LOAD MANAGEMENT STEPS

1
Historical
demand limit

2
Day of normal
load growth

3
Day of high
load growth

4
Corrective
action to
reduce rate of
rise in load

5
Period of
observation of
rate of rise of
load

Day of low load
growth
6

6   Noon   6

or rise of load in the earlier part of the day.

Sophisticated electronic equipment is available to do this (Reference 5) and compare the developing load curve with a predetermined standard. If the early increase in load takes place at an unusually rapid rate (Reference 4), corrective action can be taken early in the day to avoid exceeding the desired level of demand.

Corrective action would take the form of turning off some electrical equipment or shifting its time of operation to a less critical hour of the day. The economic incentive for such action originates with the tariff and is a part of the rate design objective.

Cost benefit balance

Most residential customers and very small commercial customers do not have electrical bills that would justify spending very large amounts on load control devices of a complex nature. However, large commercial and industrial customers can often effect substantial savings that would justify load control systems costing many thousands of dollars. Cost justification depends on how many economic factors and individual companies must usually evaluate these factors before coming to a decision.

Interruptible service

Rates may be offered that price electricity at a level below that set for firm service if the customer agrees to permit his supply of electricity to be interrupted by the utility when operating conditions on the utility's system make it advisable to do so. This may be the case during periods of abnormally high system load. It is usually done through specific instructions from the power dispatcher of the utility in accordance with special contract arrangements agreed upon in advance.

ADJUSTMENT CLAUSES

Fuel cost adjustment clauses

For many years, most utilities included in their large commercial and industrial rates a provision for varying the price per kilowatt-hour as the cost of fuel changed. These fuel cost adjustment clauses shift the price either up or down from the rate printed in the schedule by adding or subtracting a small amount arising from the change in fuel cost.

Usually the schedule stated a base price of fuel, and when the actual cost departed from the base price, an adjustment was computed. The base price was normally expressed in terms of the cost for a given number of heat units, as for example 35¢ per million Btu (British thermal units). Over a long period of time, fuel costs did not change rapidly and price adjustments were generally in the order of a few hundredths of one cent per kilowatt-hour. At that level, many customers were not very concerned when the total cost per kilowatt-hour was only one or two cents.

Impact of the energy crisis

The energy crisis of the 1970s radically changed the situation. Fuel costs rose from the modest low of 35¢ to $2.34 by 1982, per million Btu, for many utilities. Fuel cost adjustments were no longer minor adjustments to be overlooked as insignificant by many consumers but were major cost components faced by both the utility and its customers. The rapidity of the change which increased fuel costs several times over a period of about two years had a dramatic impact and fuel cost became a prime item of public interest.

Assumptions for example

The mechanism of a fuel cost adjustment provision must include a consideration of the efficiency of the utility's electric system as well as the price of fuel. To illustrate this point, consider the following:

1. Assume that the utility's generating facilities require 10,000 Btu of heat in the fuel to produce one kilowatt-hour of energy.

2. Assume that the overall transmission and distribution systems have a combined efficiency of 90%. In other words, electrical losses between the power plant and the consumer amount to 10% of the generator output.

3. Assume that the base cost of fuel as stated in the schedule is $1.90 per million Btu.

4. Assume that the current cost of fuel is $2.00 per million Btu.

Illustrative computation

Based on those assumptions, the fuel cost adjustment would be computed in the following manner:

At a generating requirement of 10,000 Btu to produce one kilowatt-hour, fuel containing one million Btu would produce 100 kilowatt-hours.

$$\frac{1,000,000 \text{ Btu}}{10,000 \text{ Btu per kwhr}} = 100 \text{ kwhr}$$

The change in cost of fuel for 1,000,000 Btu would be plus 10 cents.

$$\$2.00 - \$1.90 = \$0.10$$

Since there would be a ten-cent increase in fuel cost to produce 100 kilowatt-hours, the increase in cost for each kilowatt-hour would be one-tenth cent.

$$\frac{10¢}{100 \text{ kwhr}} = 0.1¢ \text{ kwhr}$$

However, the one-tenth cent increase per kilowatt-hour at the generating station would have to be recovered on only nine-tenths of one kilowatt-hour at the consumer's premises, after making allowance for 10% electrical losses in the transmission and distribution system.

$$90\% \text{ of } 1 \text{ kwhr} = 0.9 \text{ kwhr}$$

To collect the 0.1¢ for every 0.9 kwhr sold would require that the rate collect 0.1111 cent per kwhr billed to the customer determined as shown below:

$$\frac{0.1¢}{0.90 \text{ efficiency}} = 0.111¢ \text{ kwhr}$$

In this case, the fuel adjustment factor would be expressed as follows:

The cost per kwhr would be increased or decreased by an amount equal to the difference between the current cost of a fuel and a base cost of 190¢ per million Btu multiplied by a factor of 0.01111.

$$(200 - 190) \times 0.01111 = +0.1111¢ \text{ kwhr}$$

Thus, if the rate as stated in the schedule is 3.0¢ kwhr, the charge to the customer would be made at 3.1111¢ kwhr for the billing month involved.

This example illustrates the simplest case of fuel cost adjustment. It assumes that electricity is generated by combustion of fuels and does not give any specific consideration to hydroelectric sources of power. It does not include any consideration of power received or delivered through interconnection with other utilities. Inclusion of these factors greatly increases the complexity of the adjustment process, but the general principle is the same.

Cost of fuel is the largest single item of expense which utilities face. Consequently, the tremendous increases of the early 1970s forced utilities to re-examine carefully their existing provisions for the recovery of increases in cost of fuel. Utility companies could not have survived the impact of that crisis if fuel cost provisions had not been already present in their major tariff structures.

Today, a large majority of rate schedules include such a provision, and the concept of adjustment for cost variation has been extended to other significant areas. In many jurisdictions, some form of presentation to the commission is required each time a change is made.

Forecasting fuel cost changes

In an economic atmosphere of rapidly rising costs, the elapsed time between generation and the recovery of additional fuel cost is of vital importance.

Consequently, many adjustment clauses make provision for estimating the cost of fuel in advance of the billing month and, when the actual cost is known, for correcting the estimate in subsequent months. Various procedures to do this have been developed; and although they are complicated, utilities are convinced that "keeping current" on fuel cost recovery is absolutely essential to financial soundness.

The importance of these adjustment procedures is underscored by the fact that in 1982 the cost of fuel constituted more than 44% of utility operating expense.

Other adjustment techniques

Automatic adjustment provisions can be used for many other items of expense in addition to fuel. Adjustments may be made to incorporate changes in income taxes, sales taxes, gross receipts taxes, property taxes, and city franchise fees. An adjustment for gross receipts taxes is often incorporated in the fuel cost adjustment provisions because a change of fuel cost, if included in the customer's bill, would automatically change the amount of gross receipts tax collected.

RATE SCHEDULE MODIFIERS

Breadth of tariff coverage

Most rate schedules are designed to cover the sale of electricity to the consumer for a wide range of applications. Residential rates, for example, usually cover service for lighting, refrigeration, cooking, radio, television, and an assortment of appliances. They may or may not include large scale applications such as water heating and space heating. Air conditioning, although a large use application of service, is usually supplied under the generally applicable residential rate.

A separate consideration of large loads is often made in recognition not only of their size, but also of their dissimilarity in load characteristics to other domestic uses of electricity. They are large enough to have a formative effect on the total load served and their unique characteristics may warrant a different price per kilowatt-hour from that set forth in the basic schedule.

The end-use concept

The most direct way to assure that electricity used for a specific purpose is billed at the appropriate rate level is to write an "end-use" provision into the schedule and supply service through a separate electric meter. The term "end-use" simply refers to how the consumer uses the service. Perhaps the most familiar examples might be special rates for water heating or space heating. In many cases the "end-use" provision is set forth in a rider or supplementary provision which is appended to the schedule when such service is requested.

93

Fixed end-use blocks

When the cost of a separate meter is not economically justifiable, the special service, as in the case of water heating, may be handled by inserting a "fixed" or "floating" block on the rate schedule.

A fixed block of 500 kwhr for water-heating might be inserted in the schedule beginning at 300 kwhr and extending to 800 kwhr. Energy up to 300 kwhr and in excess of 800 kwhr would be billed at the rates set forth in the schedule. Consumption between 300 and 800 kwhr would be billed at the rate commensurate with the cost of providing service for water heating.

To illustrate the method, let us assume that such a fixed block priced at 4.0¢ kwhr has been added to hypothetical rate "A" developed in Chapter 5.

First	50 kwhr	16.0¢ kwhr
Next	50 kwhr	8.5¢ kwhr
Next	200 kwhr	7.5¢ kwhr
Next	500 kwhr	6.6¢ kwhr
Excess of	800 kwhr	6.0¢ kwhr

Minimum Bill $8.00 per month.

With this addition the rate would become the following:

First	50 kwhr	16.0¢ kwhr
Next	50 kwhr	8.5¢ kwhr
Next	200 kwhr	7.5¢ kwhr
Next	500 kwhr	4.0¢ kwhr
Next	500 kwhr	6.6¢ kwhr
Over	1,300 kwhr	6.0¢ kwhr

The inserted water heating block has been underlined for emphasis.

Under this plan the billing under the regular rate blocks of the schedule would be resumed at 800 kwhr per month, thus moving the starting point of the trailing rate to 1,300 kwhr per month. The first two rate diagrams shown in Figure 18 graphically depict this process.

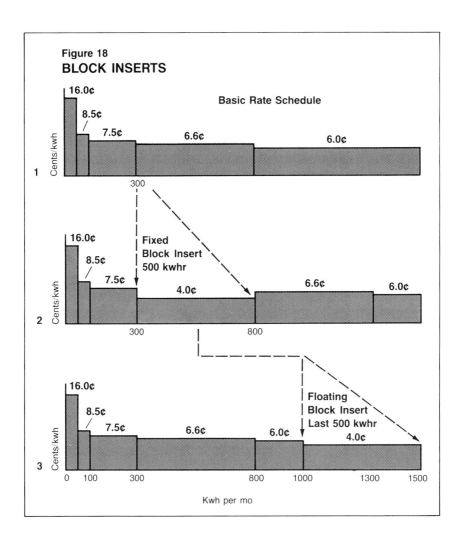

Figure 18
BLOCK INSERTS

Floating end-use blocks

A water-heating rider to the residential schedule might take a different form by adding a floating block rather than a fixed block. A floating block which takes on a varied position in the rate schedule might be described as the last 500 kwhr of monthly energy consumption which would be billed at the water-heating rate. However, the rider would also provide that it would not apply unless at least 300 kwhr per month were billed under the regular rate. The third rate diagram of Figure 18 shows the effect of a floating block of this kind.

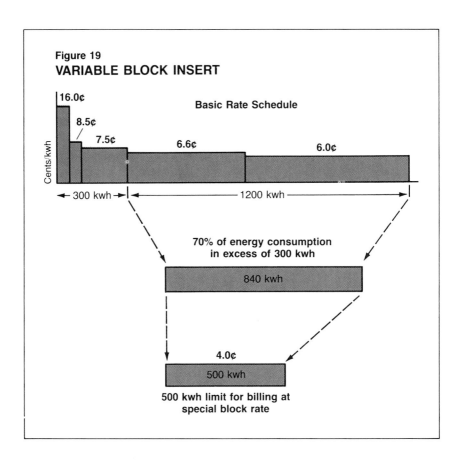

Figure 19
VARIABLE BLOCK INSERT

Percentage of use approach

Still another way of handling the water-heating service is to express the water-heating usage as a percentage of all consumption over a certain limit. For example, the schedule might provide that the water-heating rate apply to 70% of the monthly consumption which is in excess of 300 kwhr, but would also provide that it should not apply to more than 500 kwhr of assumed water-heating use. This method is depicted for a customer taking 1,500 kwhr per month in Figure 19.

With a monthly consumption of 1,500 kwhr, the customer's usage was 1,200 kwhr in excess of the 300 kwhr minimum. In accordance with the schedule, 70% of this amount would be 840 kwhr. However, the rate does not offer any special pricing for water heating use in excess of 500 kwhr. Accordingly, only 500 kwhr would have been specially priced.

If the total consumption had been 1,014 kwhr, the excess would have been 714 kwhr, and 70% of that would be 500 kwhr. Suppose the total consumption had been only 872 kwhr. The excess would have been 572 kwhr, and 70% of that amount would have been 400 kwhr. In that case, only 400 kwhr would be billed at the water-heating rate.

Stoppers

A stopper is a mechanism which may be used to limit the use of the trailing block of a declining block energy rate. This is simply a provision in the schedule that states that the average rate per kilowatt-hour for all service furnished under the schedule cannot be less than a specifically stated level.

Using Schedule A as an example the bill for 1500 kilowatt-hours would be computed as follows:

50 kwhr @	16.00¢/kwhr	....	$ 8.00
50 kwhr @	8.50¢/kwhr	....	4.25
200 kwhr @	7.50¢/kwhr	....	15.00
500 kwhr @	6.60¢/kwhr	....	33.00
700 kwhr @	6.60¢/kwhr	....	42.00
1500 kwhr			$102.25

For a consumption of 1500 kilowatt-hours the average rate would be 6.82 cents.

$$\frac{\$102.25}{1500 \text{ kwhr}} = \$ .068166$$

If the "stopper" stated that the minimum rate for all service was 6.82 cents, energy consumed in excess of 1500 kwhr per month would have been billed at the lower trailing rate of 6.00 cents were it not for the minimum average rate limitation.

Under the conditions assumed in the example, the trailing block rate of 6.00 cents would still be available for up to 700 kilowatt-hours, from 800 to 1500 kwhr, but all consumption in excess of 1500 kilowatt-hours would be billed at the "stopper" rate level of 6.82 cents per kilowatt-hour.

Ratchets

Rate schedules that include a separate demand charge often contain a provision called a "ratchet" which is included to reduce the effects of variation in monthly maximum demand.

In its simplest form, such a provision might state that the billing demand for some months, other than the peak month, should not be less than, say, 50% of that established during the peak month. The peak demand under such schedule is usually referred to as the "control demand" since the computation of the billing demand during other months may be based upon it.

Ratchet provisions vary widely from one utility to another depending upon the particular area served. They may be quite complex in rates for large commercial and industrial customers.

Other special rate provisions

In the large commercial and industrial rate categories, a number of technical provisions may apply. Some of these are penalties for low load factors, discounts for service furnished at different voltage levels, and surcharges for special equipment furnished by the utility not envisioned in the basic rate schedule.

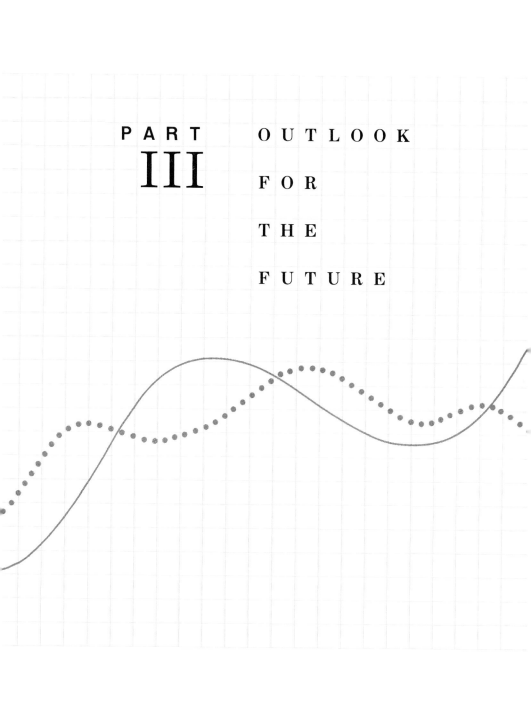

PART III

OUTLOOK FOR THE FUTURE

EMERGING TRENDS

Changes in rate concepts

The art of rate design is by no means a static discipline. Changes in rate making philosophy and technique are taking place all the time although they are not usually discernable on a day-to-day basis. By their very nature such changes are slow to surface because the effects of any basic modification in tariff must be observed over a period of several seasonal cycles, or even several years, before they can be properly evaluated. Consider, for example, air conditioning. The growth of air conditioning has had a very important role in rate design philosophy, yet it has taken more than fifty years to reach its present level. From the early days when movie theaters advertised their wares with signs that read "It's cooler inside!", air conditioning was installed by many commercial establishments and competition between those with and without cooling equipment accelerated the process.

Residential air conditioning began its climb ten or fifteen years later. Window units were relatively easy to install in both existing residences and existing commercial structures. Central air conditioning systems then became a part of nearly all new construction in areas where climatic conditions warranted.

Gradually the load characteristics of utility systems in many parts of the country shifted from winter to summer peak characteristics. This was not necessarily because of air conditioning alone but was the result of adding a major seasonal load to the customers' other aggregate needs for electricity.

At the present time, the growth of electric space heating is producing the opposite effect by adding load during winter months. Consumers who both heat and cool with electricity have a more balanced situation although the time of peak and the energy consumption for heating and cooling are not likely to be the same.

Introduction of fluorescent lamps

Throughout electric utility history new loads have continued to appear from time to time which had a major influence on rate design. Fluorescent lamps came on the market in the 1930s. They were roughly twice as efficient as the familiar incandescent lamp of that period. Some said that fluorescent lamps would cut the consumption of electricity in half since the same amount of light could be produced by half the number of kilowatt-hours. Some pessimists predicted dire consequences for the industry. Instead the new lamp provided a revolutionary light source that made it practical to raise the levels of illumination dramatically. In the 1930s, an office with an illumination level of 35 foot-candles was considered to be well lighted. Introduction of the fluorescent light source soon resulted in levels of 75 foot-candles or more for general office lighting and of several hundred foot-candles in areas where special tasks had to be performed.

Impact of ranges and water heaters

Electric ranges and electric water heaters each had an individual impact when they were introduced because the load that each added was large in comparison to the existing household load of a typical customer at that time. The typical load probably included lighting, a few appliances, and a refrigerator.

The electric water heater was one of the first devices to be operated through a time clock that kept the heating units from coming on during the utility system's peak hours. Controlled in that manner, lower "off-peak" rates could be offered for the service since it did not add to the system peak load. Yet, as time passed, the growth of automatic laundry equipment and dishwashers increased the need for hot water. Heating units were increased to improve the units' ability to recover when large quantities of water were withdrawn. Some utilities felt the need to limit the wattage of water heaters that could be connected to their system. Many reconsidered using the time clock control. During these years, other domestic loads were introduced and the water heater did not seem to loom as large, relative to the total, as it had before. All of these factors entered into any new rate design plans.

Some considered the possibility of interlocking the range and the water heater so that both could not come on the line at the same time. Today similar action is being taken by some utilities to interrupt the operation of individual air conditioning units to reduce the total peak load by decreasing the number of units in use at any one time.

These historical examples represent the more obvious past influences on rate design, other than those arising directly from industry economics. There were many more that were less apparent and the future certainly will introduce many others.

The great rate debate

For the past two decades, a critical dialogue has taken place unabated between regulators, consumers and utility personnel covering literally every phase of the electric utility rate design process. Termed the "Great Rate Debate," these discussions have clearly pointed out the increased focus of public interest in the process of putting a price tag on the product—when that product is electricity.

Criticism of declining block rates

One of the fundamental criticisms of electric tariffs was directed at the declining block energy rate. Because the price per kilowatt-hour was lower as consumption increased, critics said that the rate discouraged conservation and was wasteful in its impact. On the other hand, defenders of the rate form argue strongly that it properly reflects the cost of service, in that load characteristics at the higher consumption levels justify the lower price.

Flat and upturn rates

As divergent opinions continued to be heard, many suggested that the rate should be flattened in that the price per kilowatt-hour for the first and the last blocks of the schedule should be closer together. Others argued that they should not only be brought closer together but that the trailing block price actually should be higher than that of the preceding block, in other words, that the rate should be "inverted." Such a modification would introduce an "upturn" in price which proponents felt would discourage any tendency to waste electricity.

Seasonal rate differences

Seasonal differences in price level, designed to apply higher prices to on-peak usage came under fire because of the abrupt increase in bill that a customer experiences when he passes from an off-peak to an on-peak month.

In order to relieve such impacts, some form of budget billing could be used which spreads the higher charges as well as the lower charges, on an average basis, over a twelve month period. Such action would relieve the abrupt billing change but at the same time would lessen the price signal delivered to the consumer by the higher on-peak pricing of the schedule.

Societal considerations

Regulatory commissions have always been faced with the difficult problem of the inability of some consumers to pay bills in the amount called for by cost-based rates. Unfortunately, there is no direct correlation between cost of service and ability to pay. As a consequence, the problems of low income consumers are brought out in most rate cases.

Lifeline rates

One approach to the problem of ability to pay has been the advocacy by some of the "lifeline rate." This rate reduces the price for the first several hundred kilowatt-hours of monthly energy consumption on the assumption that it represents electricity used for basic necessities. This is a highly controversial area and serious questions are raised as to whether this discount in price does or does not primarily benefit the consumer to whom it is directed. There is much debate as to whether or not low energy consumption is synonymous with low income. Furthermore, if a discount is offered for the first several hundred kilowatt-hours, it is available to all customers. In most cases, the number of kilowatt-hours discounted is greater for the large consumers, in aggregate, than for the small-user group.

Another problem arises as to the cost responsibility for the revenue not collected because of the discount applied to the lifeline kilowatt-hours. In order to satisfy the total revenue requirements approved by commission authority, the deficiency introduced by the lifeline must be made up by other customers. The question then arises—"Should it be the responsibility of only the larger residential customers or should it be assigned to all customers other than lifeline on an across-the-board basis?"

Electric Utility Rate Design Study

Because of increasing public interest in the discipline of electric rate design, the industry responded by conducting a nationwide study, "Electric Utility Rate Design Study," which examined, in great depth, literally every facet of rate making.

In 1974, the National Association of Regulatory Utility Commissioners [NARUC] passed a resolution at its 86th annual convention requesting that the electric utility industry through the Electric Power Research Institute [EPRI] and the Edison Electric Institute [EEI] initiate "a study of the technology and cost of time-of-day metering and electronic methods of controlling peak-period usage of electricity, and also a study of the feasibility and cost of shifting various types of usage from peak to off-peak periods." Begun in response to the NARUC resolution, the study has continued since that time, and certain other investigations related to it are still in progress at the present time, (1983). More than 150 people were engaged in the original study, and input from many experts has played an important part in the undertaking. The national "Electric Rate Design Study" was a major comprehensive joint undertaking by regulators, utility personnel and consumer representatives. The findings and recommendations contained in its many reports constitute a thorough documentation of modern utility practices and will be of lasting value as a reference source.

Public Utilities Regulatory Policies Act of 1978 (PURPA)

Another major happening in the history of regulation was the passage into law of the Public Utilities Regulatory Policies Act of 1978, Titles I, II and IV which pertained to electric utilities in their entirety.

In this landmark piece of legislation, Title I dealt with retail regulatory policies of electric utilities and set forth the following objectives:

(1) To encourage conservation of energy supplied by electric utilities;
(2) To encourage the optimization of the efficiency of use of facilities and resources by electric utilities;
(3) To encourage equitable rates to electric consumers.

Within these broad objectives the law set in motion a series of actions by state regulatory commissions to review almost every facet of rate design that conceivably might come before them in a formal rate proceeding. Public hearings were to be held and specific policies were to be reviewed, considered, adopted or rejected by state bodies within certain rules contained in the legislation. This was a far reaching complex act the implementation of which is still underway in many regions of the country. The primary reason for making mention of it in this book is to point out the extensive study of rate design techniques that was undertaken in carrying out its provisions. This depth is demonstrated by the subjects to be considered under the "Standards for Electric Utilities" cited in the act which were as follows:

(1) Cost of services;
(2) Declining block rates;
(3) Time-of-day rates;
(4) Seasonal rates;
(5) Interruptible rates; and
(6) Load management techniques.

A second set of "Standards" included other basic concepts in rate design, as given below:

(1) Master metering;
(2) Automatic adjustment clauses;
(3) Information to consumers;
(4) Procedures for terminating electric services; and
(5) Advertising.

Still other sections of the act covered lifeline rates, interconnections, wheeling, power pooling, cogeneration, small power producers and other categories of utility service.

Of particular interest to the rate designer was Section 133 entitled "Gathering Information on Costs of Service" which required the collection of vast amounts of data, some of which was already available but much of which was not. Utility technical staffs were hard pressed to meet filing deadlines and in many instances additional personnel had to be employed.

In order to meet the requirements of Section 133, programs of load research had to be undertaken by utilities that had not previously established such programs. Some existing programs were expanded, and the general question of how extensive such tests should be and how frequently they should be undertaken had to be carefully evaluated in terms of the cost of additional testing.

Although marginal cost analyses were not directly required by the legislation, extensive cost information that had to be assembled and filed with the Federal Energy Regulatory Commission pertained to marginal cost concepts, and the need for that volume of information became a controversial issue.

Title II of the Act deals with a number of subjects but one of them is especially significant in the pricing of electric service. It is Section 210 entitled "Cogeneration and Small Power Production" which deals with provisions for parallel operation of small independent generating plants with the utility's system to coordinate the use of both facilities.

Rules for pricing relate to both the sales of electricity from the small generating plant to the utility and the sales at other times from the utility to the small generating entity. These rules introduce the concept of "incremental cost of alternative electric energy" which is defined as "the cost to the utility of the electric energy which, but for such purchase from such cogenerator or small power producer, such utility would generate or purchase from another source." Compliance with this provision and the computation of the "avoided cost" involved is a complex process.

ALLOCATION METHODS

As stated in Chapter 4 on "Allocation of Costs," the three methods that have gained general acceptance in retail rate regulation are the following:

Peak Responsibility
Non-Coincident Peak
Average-Excess Demand

In order to illustrate the application of each of these methods, a hypothetical utility system consisting of four classes of business has been developed. The four groups are residential, commercial, industrial, and miscellaneous. Each has been assigned a demand, energy, and other appropriate load characteristics, and these assumptions appear in Table IX. References will be made to these statistics as each of the allocation methods is discussed later in this appendix. Annual load factor for the residential class was assumed to be 33% and for commercial service 50%. Industrial class load factor was assumed to be high at 70%, and miscellaneous service was given the very low load factor of only 10%. Some exaggeration was intentional for emphasis.

Peak responsibility

Perhaps the simplest of the three methods, Peak Responsibility, also known as the Coincident Peak or CP method, allocates costs to each class of business in proportion to the contribution to the system peak made by each class of business at the time the system peak occurs. It limits the analysis to that time only. Each class may have sustained a demand at some other time even higher than its contribution to the system peak, but any other class maximum is not considered significant.

Table IX
BASIC ASSUMPTIONS FOR ILLUSTRATIVE EXAMPLE

	Annual Load Factor	Peak Demand MW	Annual Energy MWHR	Average Demand MW	Excess Demand MW	Responsibility (Contribution) to Peak
RESIDENTIAL	33%	3,000	8,760,000	1,000	2,000	2,100
COMMERCIAL	50%	4,000	17,520,000	2,000	2,000	3,200
INDUSTRIAL	70%	1,000	6,132,000	700	300	950
MISC.–OTHER	10%	500	438,000	50	450	0
		8,500	32,850,000	3,750	4,750	
SYSTEM	60%	. . . .				6,250

RATIOS (of above data)

RESIDENTIAL		0.3529	0.2667	0.2667	0.4211	0.3360
COMMERCIAL		0.4706	0.5333	0.5333	0.4211	0.5120
INDUSTRIAL		0.1177	0.1867	0.1867	0.0631	0.1520
MISC.–OTHER		0.0588	0.0133	0.0133	0.0947	0.0000
		1.0000	1.0000	1.0000	1.0000	1.0000

	[1]Weighted Average Factor	Weighted Excess Factor	Average Excess Factor
RESIDENTIAL	0.1600	0.1684	0.3284
COMMERCIAL	0.3200	0.1684	0.4884
INDUSTRIAL	0.1120	0.0253	0.1373
MISC.–OTHER	0.0080	0.0379	0.0459
	0.6000	0.4000	1.0000

[1] Average Demand Factors weighted at System Load Factor Level of 60 percent.

Figure 20 illustrates the Peak Responsibility application to the hypothetical case. Allocation factors are given for each class in proportion to the demand involved. Note that the Miscellaneous Group was assumed to use electricity entirely on an off-peak basis, and consequently assumed no share of responsibility for creating the system peak. Street lighting, for example, would in most cases fall into such a category. However, on the system of a winter peaking utility, street lighting would probably peak during the system peak load period.

By confining the analysis to the component parts of the system peak, the method does not consider class energy consumption and class load factor. It does give consideration to coincidence of demand. The major attribute of the Peak Responsibility method is its basic simplicity.

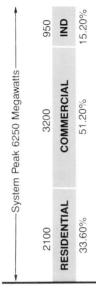

Figure 20
PEAK RESPONSIBILITY METHOD

Also known as the "COINCIDENT-PEAK" or "C–P" method, this method allocates costs to each class of business in proportion to the contribution to the system peak made by that class *at the time the peak occurs*.

Measurement is confined to a single day and therefore ignores load conditions existing on days other than the day of maximum system demand.

Allocation factors for the hypothetical case used for purposes of illustration are as follows:

Residential Service	2100 MW	.3360
Commercial Service	3200 MW	.5120
Industrial Service	950 MW	.1520
Miscellaneous	0 MW	.0000
	6250 MW	1.0000

Miscellaneous Service was assumed to be completely off of the system peak and therefore was not assigned any peak responsibility under this method.

Non-coincident class peak

In contrast to the Peak Responsibility approach, the Non-Coincident Peak or NCP method treats each class of business as a separate entity, independent of other classes served by the utility. The allocation of costs is based on the maximum demand established by each class of business, at any time during the period under study, without regard to whether it coincides with the system peak or with the peak demand of the other classes of business.

These nonrelated class peaks are added together arithmetically, and the allocation factors relate each class peak to the arithmetic sum of the peaks obtained by that addition.

In contrast to Peak Responsibility, Non-Coincident Peak methodology does give some consideration to class load factor but assigns the benefits of interclass diversity in proportion to class peak demands.

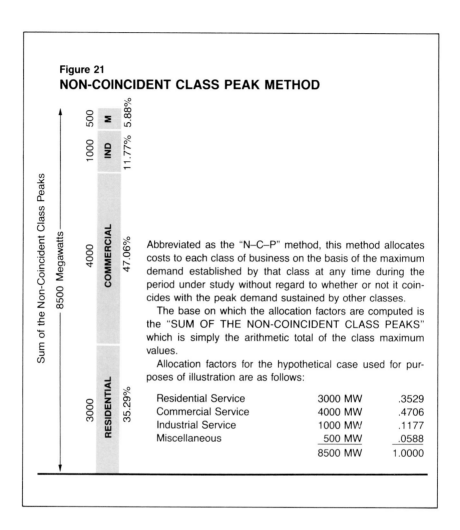

Figure 21
NON-COINCIDENT CLASS PEAK METHOD

Abbreviated as the "N–C–P" method, this method allocates costs to each class of business on the basis of the maximum demand established by that class at any time during the period under study without regard to whether or not it coincides with the peak demand sustained by other classes.

The base on which the allocation factors are computed is the "SUM OF THE NON-COINCIDENT CLASS PEAKS" which is simply the arithmetic total of the class maximum values.

Allocation factors for the hypothetical case used for purposes of illustration are as follows:

Residential Service	3000 MW	.3529
Commercial Service	4000 MW	.4706
Industrial Service	1000 MW	.1177
Miscellaneous	500 MW	.0588
	8500 MW	1.0000

Figure 21 shows the application of the NCP procedure in the hypothetical case.

Average-excess demand

Use of the "average demand" is made to determine the amount by which the "class peak demand" exceeds the average. This produces a measure of performance termed the "excess demand" which, like load factor, relates to the extent to which the utility's facilities are used by the consumer. The Average-Excess Demand, or AED method, is by far the most complex of the three procedures.

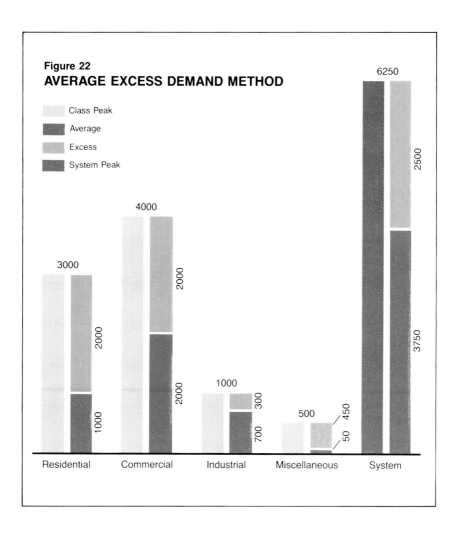

Figure 22
AVERAGE EXCESS DEMAND METHOD

Legend:
- Class Peak
- Average
- Excess
- System Peak

Residential: 3000 (Excess 2000, System Peak 1000)
Commercial: 4000 (Excess 2000, Average 2000)
Industrial: 1000 (Excess 300, 700)
Miscellaneous: 500 (450, 50)
System: 6250 (2500, 3750)

Figures 22 and 23 show the basic elements for each class of business, and for the system. Each peak demand is separated into the average and excess values. Average demand is simply that level of load that would have been experienced if service had been delivered on a uniform basis, instead of on a varying basis as is actually the case. Excess demand is the amount obtained by subtracting the average demand from the peak demand. Values for each of these components are given on the chart and are shown graphically as well. The ratio of excess demand to average demand is also shown for each class of business, and is a measure of non-uniformity in the load pattern; the class with greatest non-uniformity has the lowest load factor and vice-versa.

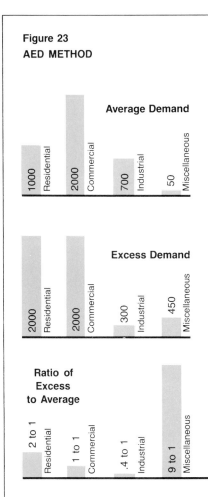

Figure 23
AED METHOD

Average Demand

1000 Residential
2000 Commercial
700 Industrial
50 Miscellaneous

Excess Demand

2000 Residential
2000 Commercial
300 Industrial
450 Miscellaneous

Ratio of
Excess
to Average

2 to 1 Residential
1 to 1 Commercial
.4 to 1 Industrial
9 to 1 Miscellaneous

"AVERAGE DEMAND" is that level of demand which would have been sustained if the same number of kilowatt-hours as actually consumed had been delivered on a uniform 24 hour a day around the clock basis instead of being supplied on the varying pattern experienced in actual practice. It is the least level of load under which that number of kilowatt-hours could be transmitted to the customer. It is arithmetically proportioned to the energy consumption.

"EXCESS DEMAND" is the number of kilowatts by which the actual peak demand exceeds the "AVERAGE DEMAND". As such it is a measure of how much the actual demand departs from the minimum load level required to deliver the same energy on a uniform or constant delivery basis.

By relating the "EXCESS DEMAND" to the "AVERAGE DEMAND" the ratio gives a measure of the degree of variation in the consumers load. In the illustrative example the Industrial Class with the highest annual load factor (70%) has the lowest E/A Ratio, namely 0.4 to 1. On the other hand the Miscellaneous Group with an annual load factor of only 10% has the highest E/A Ratio of the four classes at 9 to 1.

Referring back to Table IX, columns 4 and 5 give the statistics for average and excess demands. Values in megawatts are given in the top section, and the allocation ratios are given in the middle section. In the lower section of the table, the ratios for average demand are given a weight of 60%; the system load factor and the excess demands are weighted at 40% to produce an average excess factor based on that combination.

By assigning a value to the average cost component equal to the system load factor, the same degree of significance is applied to average demand for each class as is present for the system as a whole. Load factor may be computed in several ways, and in analyzing the AED method, it is appropriate to consider the following relationship:

$$\text{Load Factor} = \frac{\text{Average Demand}}{\text{Maximum Demand}}$$

The average-excess method considers both load factor and diversity although it does not directly incorporate the share of system peak statistics.

INDEX